Architectural Perspective Grids

Architectural Perspective Grids

Three-Dimensional Design and Perspective Construction Simplified

John S. M. Chen, AIA

William T. Cooper, AIA

McGraw-Hill

New York   San Francisco   Washington, D.C.   Auckland   Bogotá
Caracas   Lisbon   London   Madrid   Mexico City   Milan
Montreal   New Delhi   San Juan   Singapore
Sydney   Tokyo   Toronto

Library of Congress Cataloging-in-Publication Data

Chen, John S. M.
    Architectural perspective grids : three-dimensional design and
perspective construction simplified / John S. M. Chen, William T. Cooper.
       p.   cm.
    ISBN 0-07-011133-2 (hardcover)
    1. Architectural drawing. 2. Perspective. I. Cooper, William T.
II. Title.
NA2710.C46   1995
720'.28'4—dc20   95-45340
                                                      CIP

McGraw-Hill
A Division of The McGraw·Hill Companies

1 2 3 4 5 6 7 8 9 0   EDW/EDW   9 0 0 9 8 7 6 5

PN 0-07-011660-1
PART OF
ISBN 0-07-011133-2

The sponsoring editor for this book was Wendy Lochner, the editing supervisor was Jane Palmieri, and the production supervisor was Pamela Pelton. It was set in Palatino by Renee Lipton of McGraw-Hill's Professional Book Group composition unit.

This book is printed on acid-free paper.

Contents

Preface

Our habits of architectural design are generally developed at a young age. Most of us have been taught to design a building from floor plans to elevations and sections. If time and budget allow, we construct an isometric drawing, a perspective, or build a model. Some of our designs never actually reach the three-dimensional stage. Given that everything we see is in three dimensions and our designs are so often in two dimensions, an enormous gap exists between the design and its potential reality. Educators and architects so far have tended to use two-dimensional rather than three-dimensional tools because of the time factor and the special expertise required to explore design issues using three-dimensional tools.

Can we draw a perspective without floor plans, elevations, and sections? Can we design a building in three dimensions before we do it in two dimensions? Can we integrate all views of a building into one coherent entity of design? The answer to all these questions is yes, but with adequate technology.

In recent years, the rapid development of computers and of three-dimensional software packages is changing all aspects of architectural design. The use of these essential new tools has affected the way in which architects explore design issues. Today, more designs are done in three dimensions than ever before. The architectural profession is about to experience an explosion in the utilization of computer technology in every aspect of architectural practice. The computer is now not only a drafting tool, but also a design tool. Computers can both draw construction documents and generate sophisticated forms. Some of these forms are considered almost impossible to generate manually. Therefore, the computer is not just another drafter's tool; it is a very smart tool. World-renowned architects such as Peter Eisenman and Frank Gehry have forged computer links to the very early stages of design. Eisenman

begins with a philosophy for his design and transfers it mathematically; then he lets the computer construct the two- and three-dimensional results of the mathematical expression. Gehry normally does his three-dimensional designs in another way: He uses the traditional modeling method and then translates the dramatic and irregular shapes of the building models to computer drawings via a digitizer.

Although these two approaches are very effective, there exists still another approach to the exploration of three-dimensional design—the use of architectural perspective grids proposed here. These architectural perspective grids are also called *three-dimensional design grids*. They enable us to combine the use of the computer with the use of traditional hand-drawn sketches. Using the three-dimensional grids, the user is actually designing the perspective, floor plan, elevations, and sections simultaneously and compositely. He or she would hardly ever need to use triangles, T squares, or other instruments. Since the grids are self-explanatory and very easy to use, the time spent on the design can be greatly reduced.

The other use for these grids is to prepare presentations—to construct perspectives from floor plans, elevations, and sections. The perspective drawing is the most difficult drawing in descriptive geometry, yet the most useful drawing in architectural presentation; it is also the most realistic three-dimensional drawing compared to axonometric and oblique drawings. The conventional way of doing hand-constructed perspectives suffers from a number of disadvantages, such as the time consumption factor. Sometimes the vanishing points of the object land at an unreachable distance, and we do not always have a big enough space to construct the perspective. To overcome these disadvantages, the grid system was invented long before computers were ever used for design and drafting purposes. Early perspective grids provided limited angles to choose from. They were also not very accurate because of their conventional hand construction. Most were designed for general use in graphic arts rather than for the specific purposes of architecture.

The development and application of the computer in the field of architectural design and presentation have been so rapid that today computers are used both to generate perspective wire frames and to draw the finished color renderings. But up until this day, the process is still time-consuming. To simplify the process, we can use the computer to first generate a series of grids and then plot all the details manually on the grid to produce the perspective wire frame. By doing so we not only save time but also offer people with little or no computer knowledge an easy method of perspective construction.

This book contains a series of computer-generated grids especially designed for architecture. The grids can be used by professionals and students of architecture, urban planning, interior design, landscape architecture, and other environmental design disciplines. They can be used for three-dimensional design or perspective constructions. More than 120 architectural perspective grids with different angles, station points, and eye levels designed for exterior perspectives, interior perspectives, bird's-eye views, taller buildings, and three-point perspectives are included. They can be used for individual buildings as well as group buildings. Step-by-step examples of how to use these grids are given in the different chapters on the various sorts of perspective grids. An accompanying DOS disk in DXF file format which facilitates the use of custom perspective grids enables users to plot them in any size preferred.

John Chen
William T. Cooper

Acknowledgments

For sharing their wealth of knowledge and information with us, we are most indebted to our fellow professors and architects. While the inspiration and encouragement came from many sources, special energy was received from Prof. José Mapily and other professors who believe that three-dimensional design should play an important role in architectural education and practice. These professors helped to test the different computer-generated grids in their design studios where they train students in the methods of architectural design.

We would like to express our appreciation to those students who have used these grids in their own creative ways and gave constructive suggestions for this book.

We are also very grateful to Dean Harry Robinson III, Associate Dean Katherine Prigmore, and Department Chairman Victor Diedzienyo of the School of Architecture and Planning at Howard University. Without their constant support and encouragement, this book would not be a reality.

Special acknowledgment goes to our senior editors, Joel Stein and Wendy Lochner, for backing the concept of the book and for supervising the entire process. We also wish to thank Gemma Veltan and Golden Hung of McGraw-Hill International for their time and effort in negotiating a possible Chinese version of this book.

Our gratitude extends to Diane Cooper for her continuous assistance, editing, and everyday support in putting this book together.

Finally, this book is dedicated to all the architects, landscape architects, interior designers, and students of environmental design who are now making the transition from manual design to electronic design, from two-dimensional design to three-dimensional. We hope this book can provide a link and forge this transition.

Basic Methodology

In manual perspective construction, shown in Fig. 1-1, we need to rotate the floor plan (or sometimes the roof plan) to a certain angle to establish its relationship to the picture plane (PP); then we determine the location of the station point (SP). From SP we draw two lines parallel to AB and AD that intersect the picture plane at P and Q. From the station point we also draw lines toward D and B, which will intersect the picture plane at K and L, respectively. All these are seen on the plan view of the object. Our next step is to draw a ground line (GL) and measure a distance from the ground line to determine the horizon line (HL). Since AE is on the picture plane, we can just measure a true height (TH) from the ground line to determine the height of AE and connect lines from A and E to vanishing points VP1 and VP2, which were projected perpendicularly down from P and Q. From K and L project perpendicular lines until they intersect the tapered lines at D, B, F, and H. Thus we have completed the perspective construction.

In Fig. 1-1 the only time we can measure a line is when that line is on the picture plane. In this case it is the dotted line ST. It is called the *measuring line* (ML). In a manual perspective construction, there can be more than one measuring line, depending on how many times the object intersects the picture plane. In Fig. 1-2 we divide an object into equal increments. These increments do not have a scale; it is up to the user to give them a scale. Let's assign 2'0" to each increment; now no matter where we look at it, each increment will be 2'0", either horizontally or vertically. Here not only is AE measurable, but also everything on planes ABCD, ABFE, and ADHE, is measurable. We call these planes *measuring planes* (MPs). As a result of dividing the object into equal increments, there are more tapered lines to follow, and we can really get rid of all the elements that helped to create the perspective grids, including vanishing points, and just leave the grid system to be used.

In Fig. 1-3 we show an example of plotting an object (building) when all the changing points of the object are on the measuring planes. In this case we assign 5'0" to each increment. Let's say the horizon line is 15'0" from the ground; just count 3 increments down to draw lines EF and FG. Line EF is 35'0" from the corner to the left; we just count 7 increments, and we get to the 35'0" mark. We can draw all the rest of the lines in the same manner. We cannot draw a slanted line directly on a measuring plane such as BC, but we can locate its two end points B and C on the measuring plane and connect B and C, and then we have drawn BC.

In Fig. 1-4 we show how to construct a slanted plane ABDC that is not on the measuring planes. We can locate its related points A, B, C, and D on the left and right measuring planes and then connect A and B as well as C and D. Thus we have constructed the slanted plane. The other points of this object are all on the measuring plane; we can just count the increments or relate them to the dimension marks and have the perspective completed.

In Fig. 1-5 we show how to construct a point B that is not on the measuring planes. We can construct it by using only vertical measuring planes or with the help of a floor measuring plane. First we draw the elevations of the object (building) on the left and right measuring planes; at the same time we locate the projections (locations) of B on the left measuring plane (shown here as A) and on the right measuring plane (shown as C). Using a pin at A, rotate a triangle around this fixed point A until one side of the triangle is between two tapered lines on the right measuring plane; draw a line that seems to be vanishing into the same vanishing point of those two tapered lines. From C use the same method to draw a tapered line following the tapered lines on the left measuring plane; the intersection of the tapered lines from A and C occurs at B. This method might not be very accurate when angle ABC is approaching 180°. In this situation a floor measuring plane (floor grid) will be very handy. Just pump up B vertically from its location on the floor measuring plane and intersect either of the two previously mentioned tapered lines, and

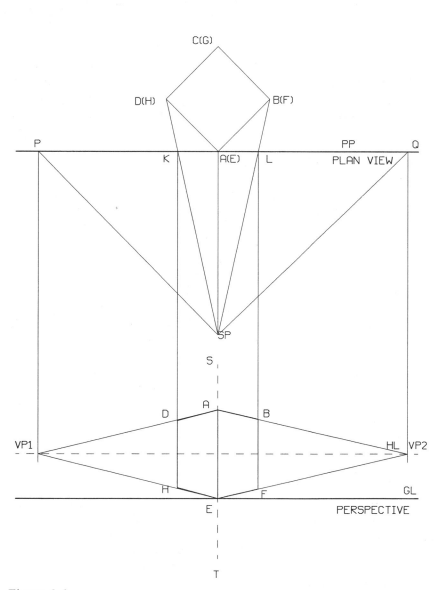

Figure 1-1

Figure 1-2

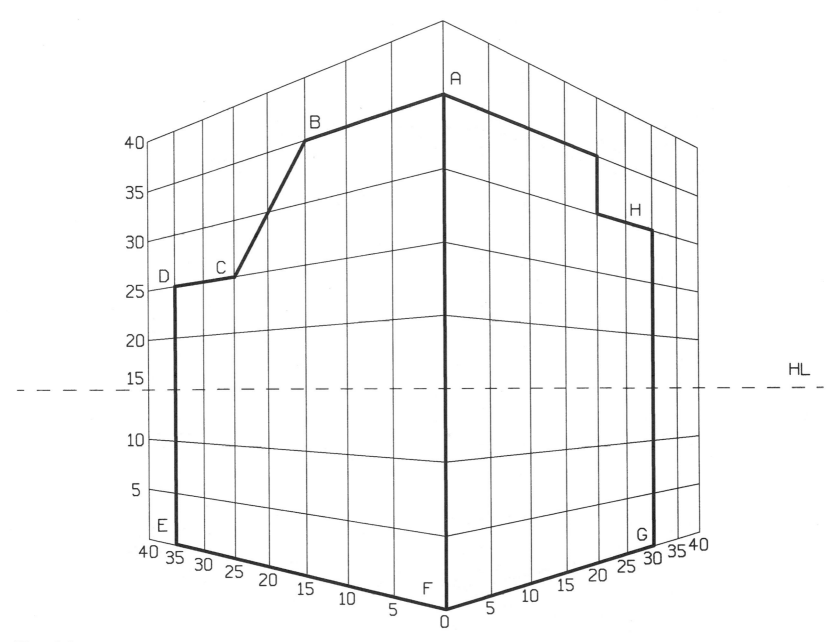

Figure 1-3

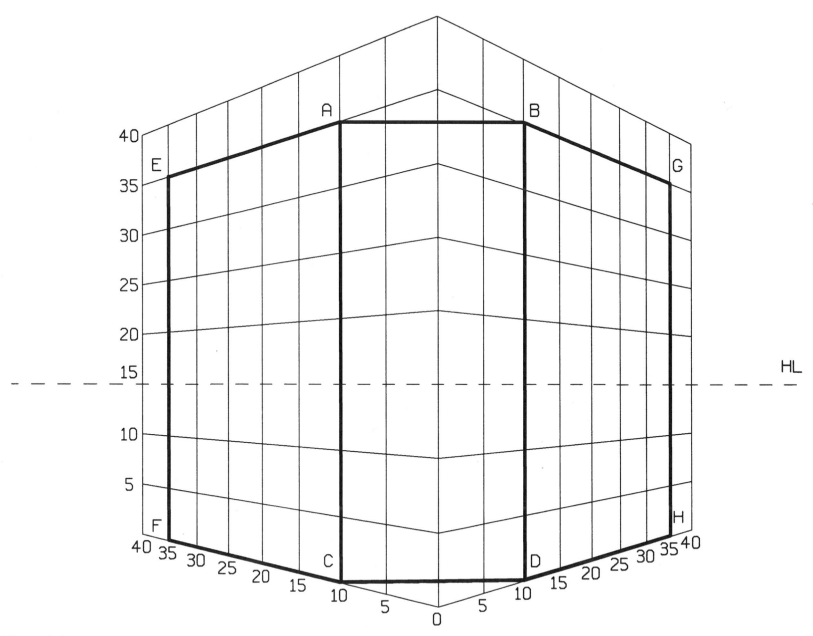

Figure 1-4

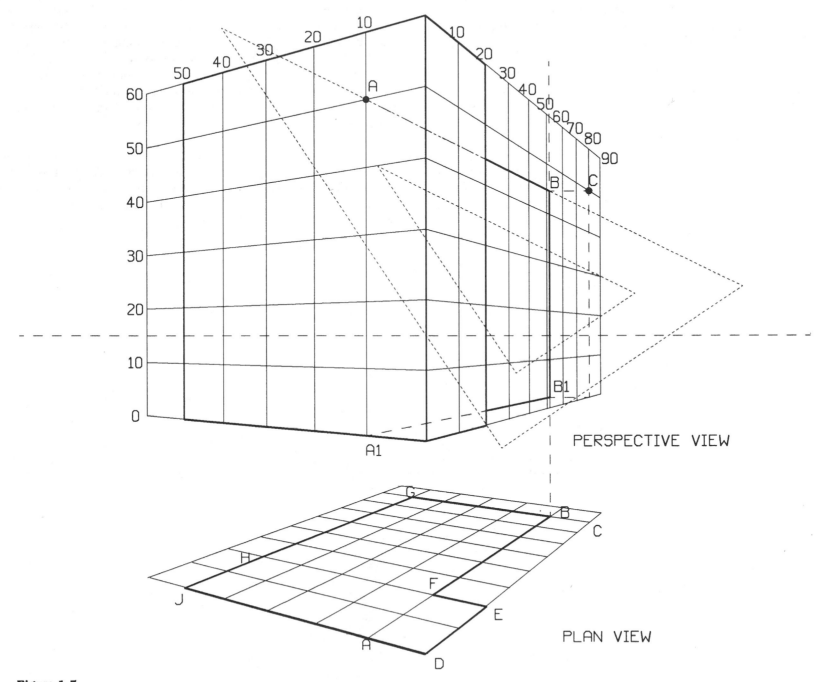

PERSPECTIVE VIEW

PLAN VIEW

Figure 1-5

the location of B in the perspective is determined. We can use the same method to locate B1, which is at the lower part of the building. Then the rest of the building can be easily constructed by the method just described.

Figure 1-6 shows how to construct a cylindrical shape. First we draw a square around the floor plan of the circle and make all its sides tangent to the circle. Then we divide the square into as many increments as we want. In this example we divided the square into six increments along each side, thus forming a grid. This grid will intersect the circle at 20 points. Find a perspective grid, use the same number of increments, and approximately plot the locations of these 20 points on both the top measuring plane and the floor measuring plane; connect the utmost edge of the upper and lower circles with two vertical lines, and we have constructed a cylinder.

Actually we can construct all kinds of irregular shapes with this method. Figure 1-7 shows how to construct an irregularly shaped cone. One side of the base plan of the cone is a rectangle, and the other side is an irregularly shaped curve. The location of peak point A is also shown on the base plan. Construct a grid around the base plan. Find a perspective grid suitable for the purpose, and plot the related points 1 to 11 on the floor measuring plane. Locate peak point A on the top measuring plane. Connect the related points to point A, and we have constructed this irregularly shaped cone.

Because of limited space, this book cannot include all the examples of how to construct various shapes of structures. We would like users to get familiar and experiment with these grids. By doing so you can find the most effective way of implementing these grids for your design and presentation.

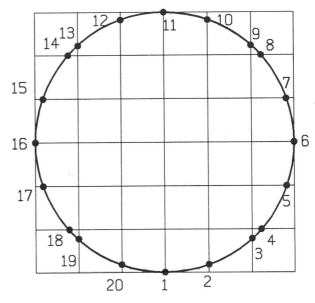

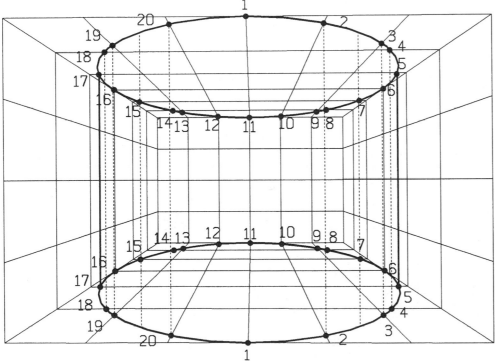

Figure 1-6

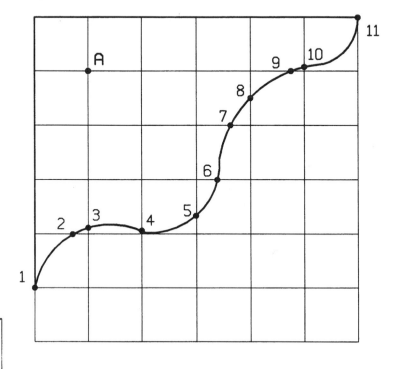

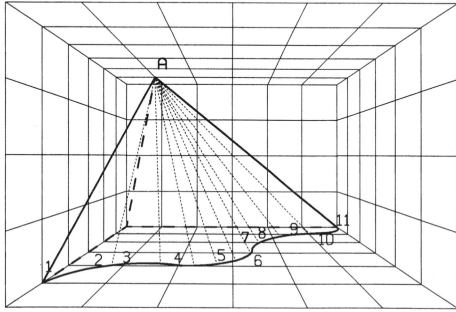

Figure 1-7

Perspective Grids for Site Design and Presentation

The most useful grids for three-dimensional design are the site grids. Each site grid is normally composed of a horizontal (floor) measuring plane and two or three vertical measuring planes. As we can see, in a site grid the horizontal measuring plane is at a more tilted angle. Here we can clearly see the floor plan, the entourage as well as its relationship with the related elevations on the vertical measuring planes. We can start the design without using a T square, triangle, or scale. Knowing the configuration and size of the lot, the floor-area ratio (FAR) of the building (or buildings), and other code requirements, we can start the three-dimensional design immediately.

The first example is a three-dimensional design of a furniture warehouse done by student Edward Lomax of Prof. José Mapily's Design 3 Studio of Howard University, School of Architecture and Planning. Instead of designing the furniture store from two-dimensional floor plans and elevations, he designed it directly on a three-dimensional site grid. The grid itself does not have a scale; it is up to the user to assign a scale to the grid, and in this case each increment equals 5'0". Now the user can plot the property line. After calculating the FAR, the user decided that the footprint of the building is approximately 110'0" by 90'0". Step 1 (Fig. 2-1) is to plot the two-dimensional site, floor plan, and elevations on the floor and vertical measuring planes. The location of the floor plan is determined by meeting all setback requirements and leaving enough space for parking, traffic, and adequate landscaping. In this manner he sketched the entire footprint of the site on the floor measuring plane. Actually a very detailed floor plan can be designed on the floor measuring plane if it is necessary. In this example we are only trying to explain how all aspects of design can be done simultaneously, and the details of the floor plan can actually be worked out later. After plot-

ting on the floor measuring plane, the user can start to plot the related elevations on the vertical measuring planes.

Now is the time to pump up the different heights of the building. For instance, if the user wants to find the height of AB, he or she can just draw a vertical line from B and a tapered line from C following the direction of the tapered line on the floor measuring plane. When the two lines intersect, the location of point A is determined. Actually all the different heights of the building are determined by relating the locations of these points on the floor and vertical measuring planes. In step 2 (Fig. 2-2), when all heights of the building have been decided, the three-dimensional image of the building will start to appear on the perspective grid, and then the user can draw in the trees, cars, people, streetlights, etc. Everything here is drawn to a quite accurate scale and is measurable. Here the user is not doing the drawings one by one, but is tying the floor plan, site plan, elevations, and perspective into one design entity. The student also added some shade and shadows to make the drawing look more realistic.

The second example constructs a bird's-eye view of a residential complex with the site grid from an existing site plan and some elevation information. The site is 530'0" by 490'0" and is located in Israel. These housing units are for new immigrants, and they are relatively small units. Figure 2-3 shows a partial site plan, each block contains 12 units, and they have exits from the front and back of the buildings. The easiest way to construct a bird's-eye view is to put a grid on the partial site plan first; in this case each increment represents 10'0". In our example the buildings are simple rectangular shapes, but the user will find this method also useful when the configuration of the building is a complex shape, such as a diagonal or curvilinear shape, because any shape com-

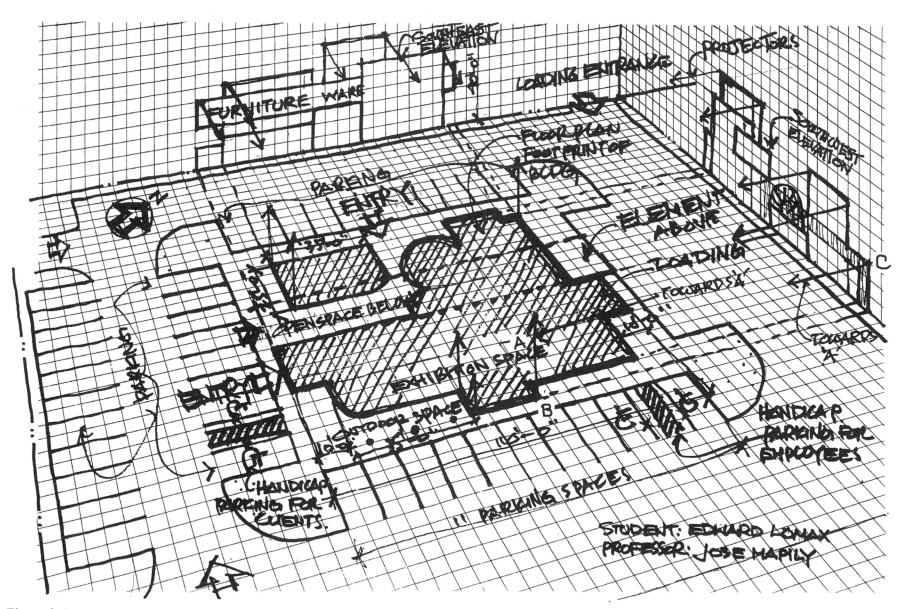

Figure 2-1

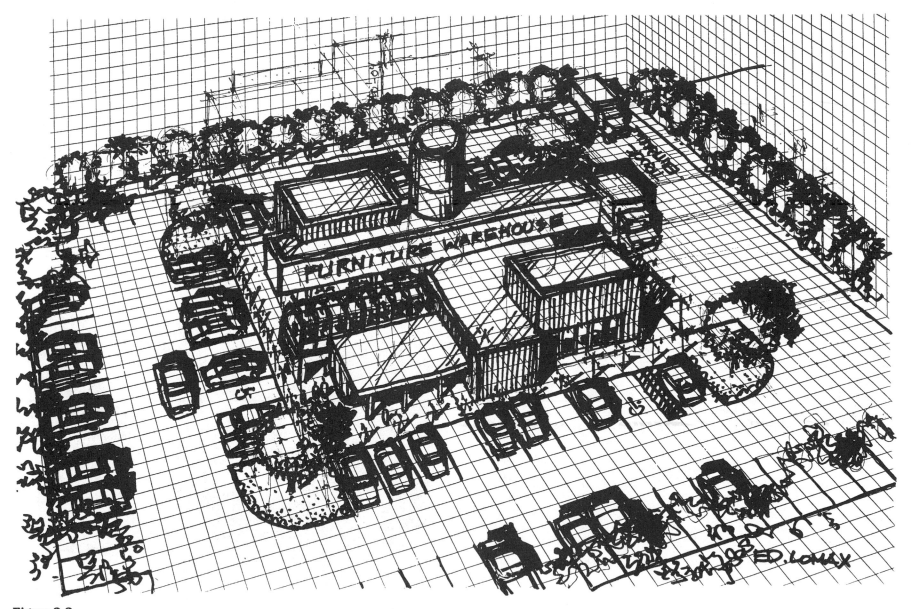

FURNITURE WAREHOUSE

ED.LOMAX

Figure 2-2

prises points which relate to the X and Y axes, as mentioned in Chap. 1. Figure 2-4 shows the exterior appearance of a four-unit complex of this project. Keep in mind that these two-story housing units are approximately 20'0" tall.

Now we can start to construct the bird's-eye view of the site. Step 1 (Fig. 2-5) is to divide the site into housing blocks, communal areas, and circulation areas. Step 2 (Fig. 2-6) is to plot two-dimensional details of the

housing blocks and the whole site on the floor measuring plane. The configuration of the community center in this example was made up. We also draw a swimming pool and a basketball court next to the community center. Then we draw in the roads and parking spaces. Locations of important trees are marked with an X. To find the heights of the buildings, we need to use the two vertical measuring planes. For instance, to find point A, we must draw a line from A' following the direction of the

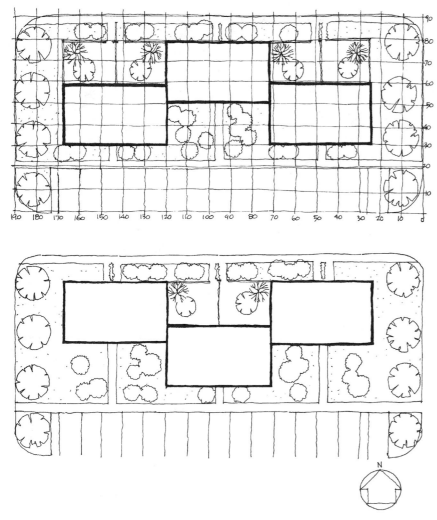

Figure 2-3

Figure 2-4

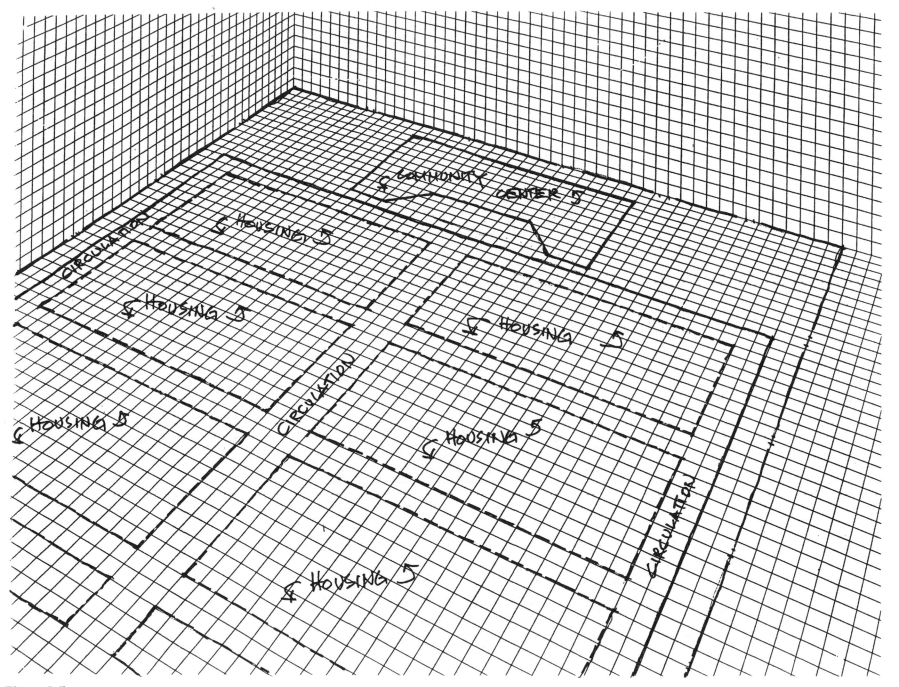

Figure 2-5

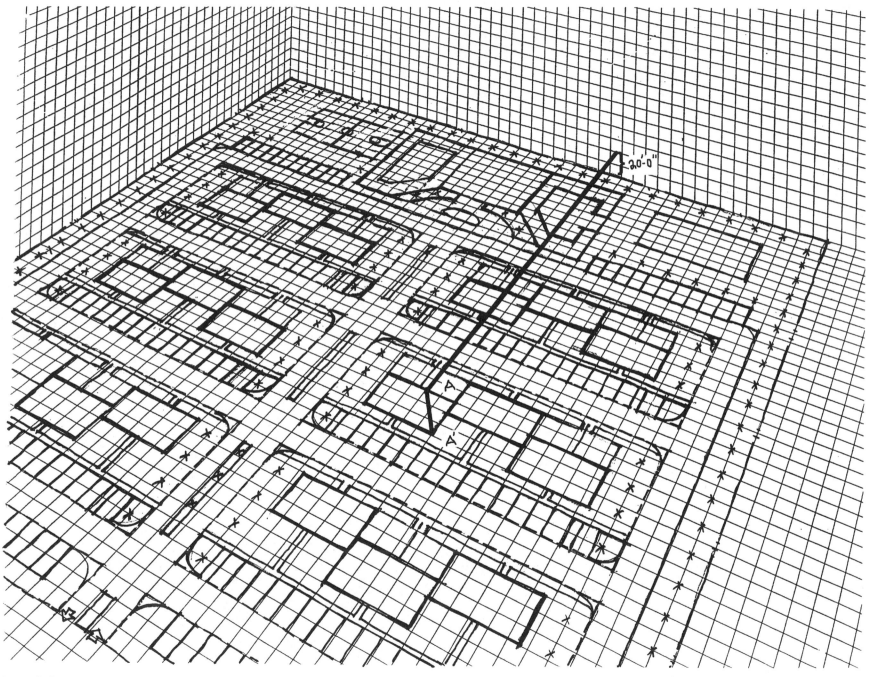

20'-0"

Figure 2-6

tapered lines on the floor measuring plane until it reaches the intersection of the floor measuring plane and the vertical measuring plane; we measure up 2 increments, which equals 20'0", and draw another line from the 20'0" point back along the related tapered lines until it intersects AA' at A. We then extend up all the other heights, using the same method. Figure 2-7 is the finished bird's-eye view of the site. When we plot the exterior of the housing units, we use Fig. 2-4 as a reference. The community center was added.

Using this method, we can construct a bird's-eye perspective without using any sophisticated instrument and save a lot of time compared to the manual perspective construction method.

Following are 20 grids, similar to the figures referred to within the chapter text, for use in creating site perspectives and three-dimensional design. Additional grids with varying angles can be found on the book's accompanying computer disk in the Bird's-eye DXF files. Refer to Chap. 6 for information on how to access these additional grids.

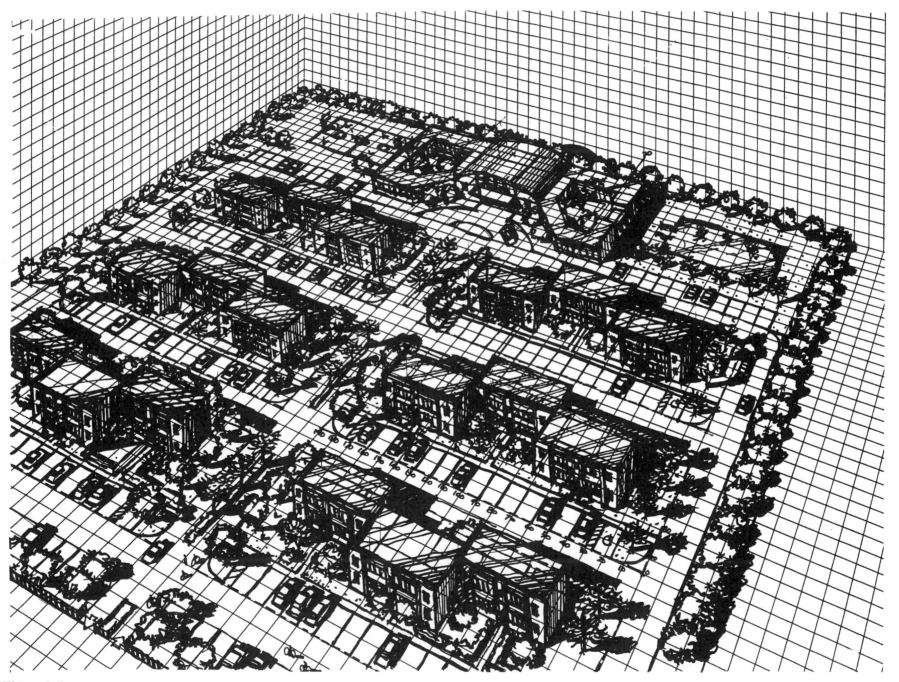

Figure 2-7

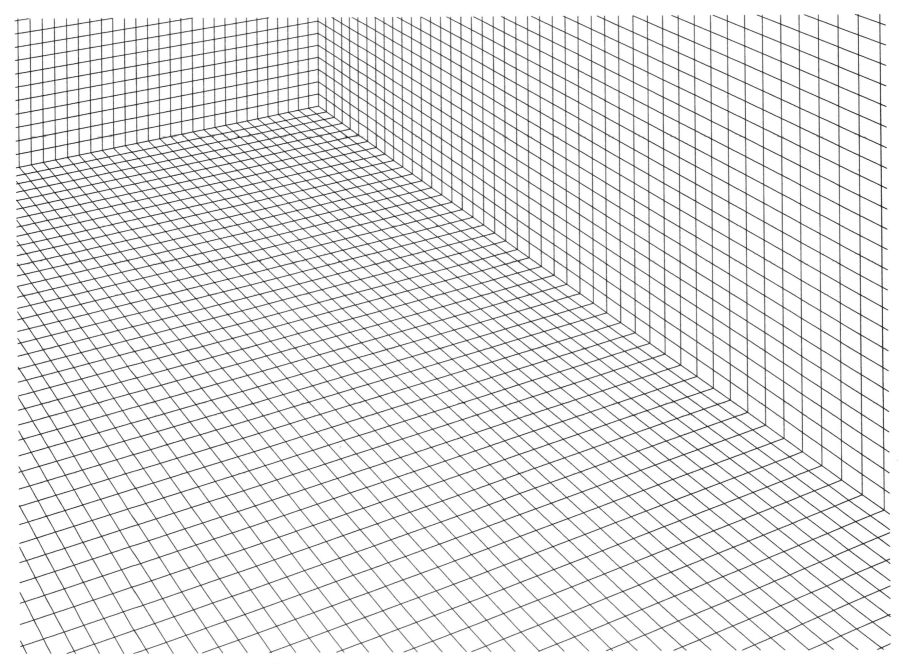

Bird's-eye view example 1, view 1, horizon line 100.

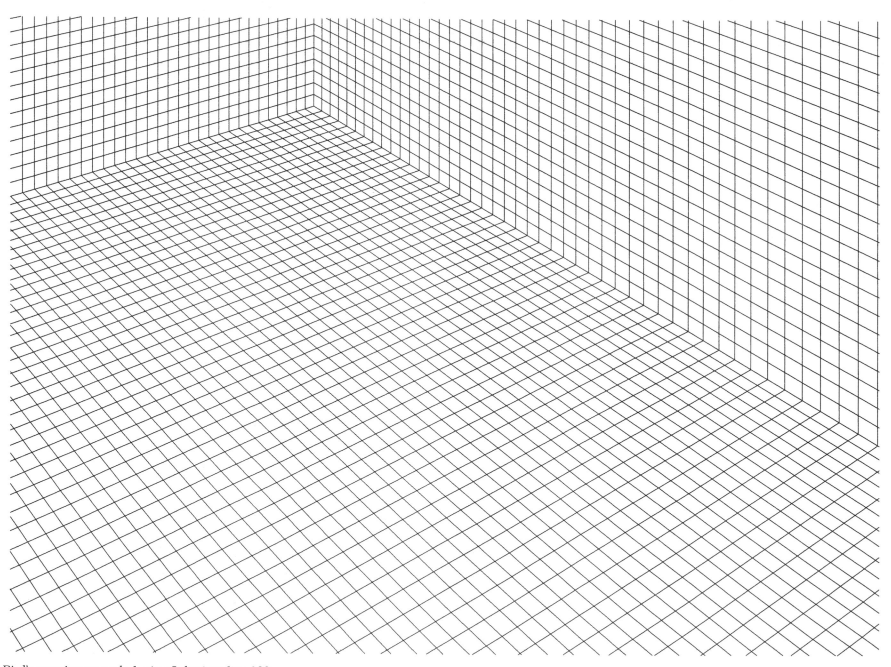

Bird's-eye view example 1, view 2, horizon line 100.

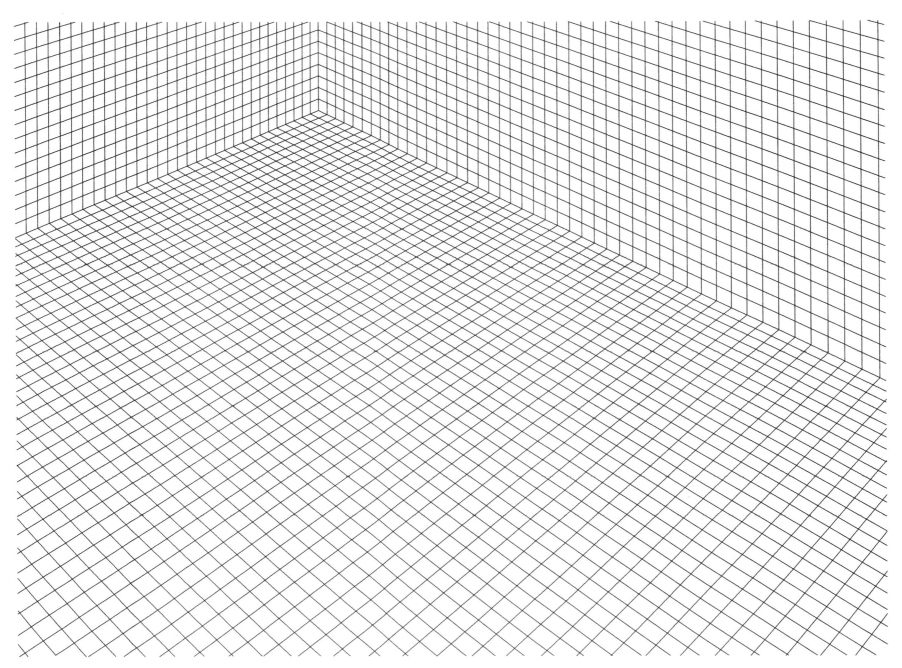

Bird's-eye view example 1, view 3, horizon line 100.

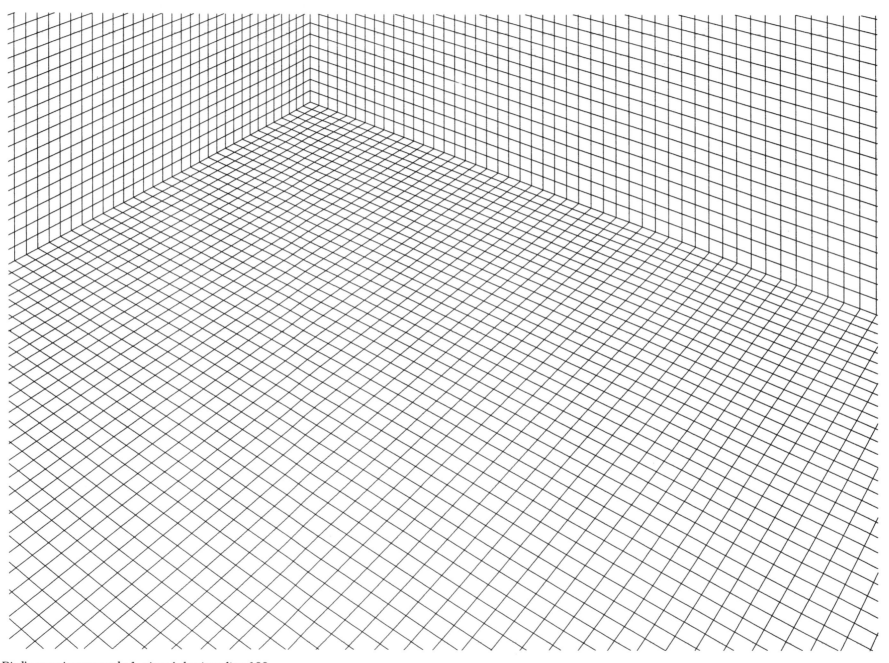

Bird's-eye view example 1, view 4, horizon line 100.

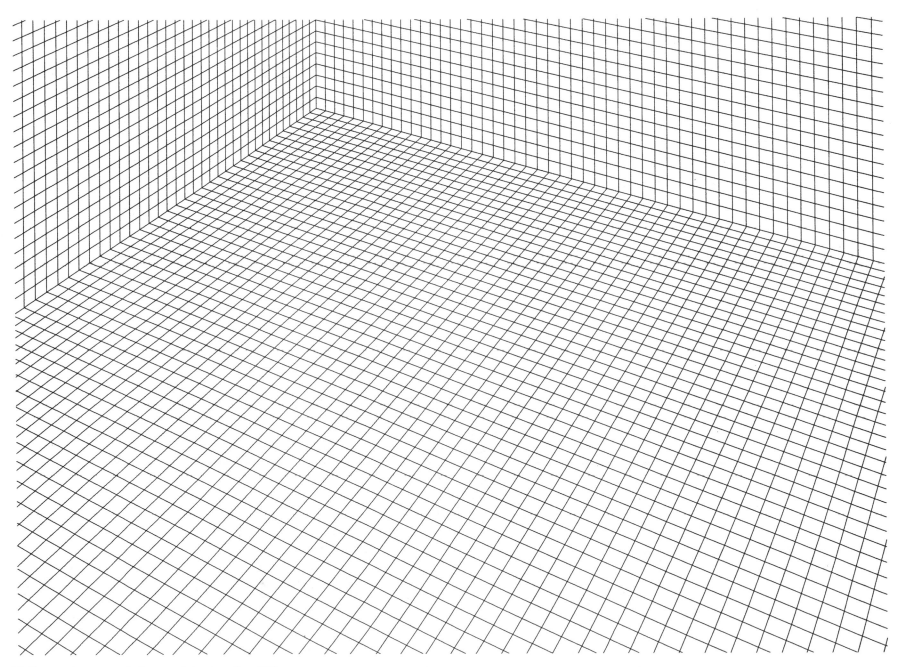

Bird's-eye view example 1, view 5, horizon line 100.

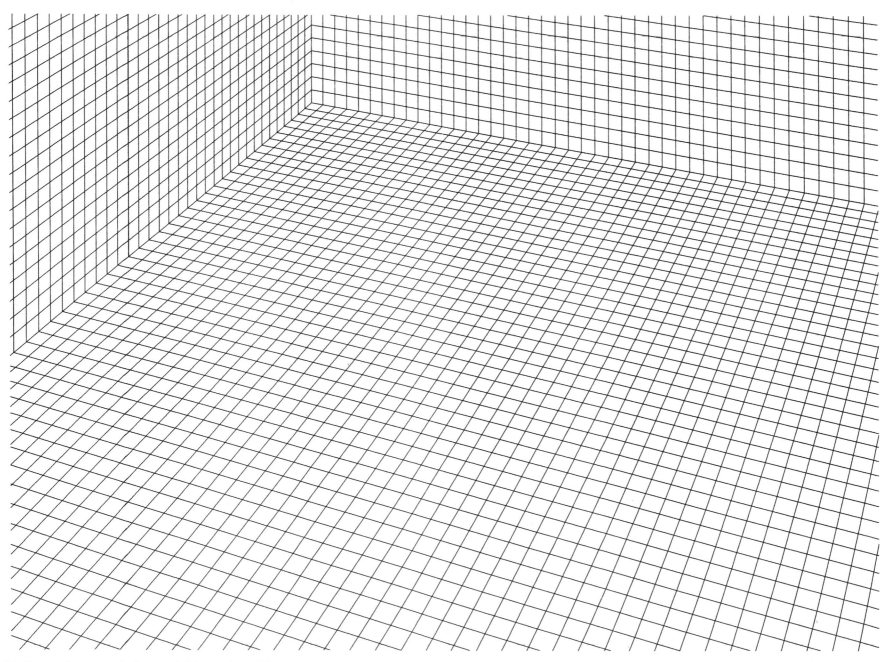

Bird's-eye view example 1, view 6, horizon line 100.

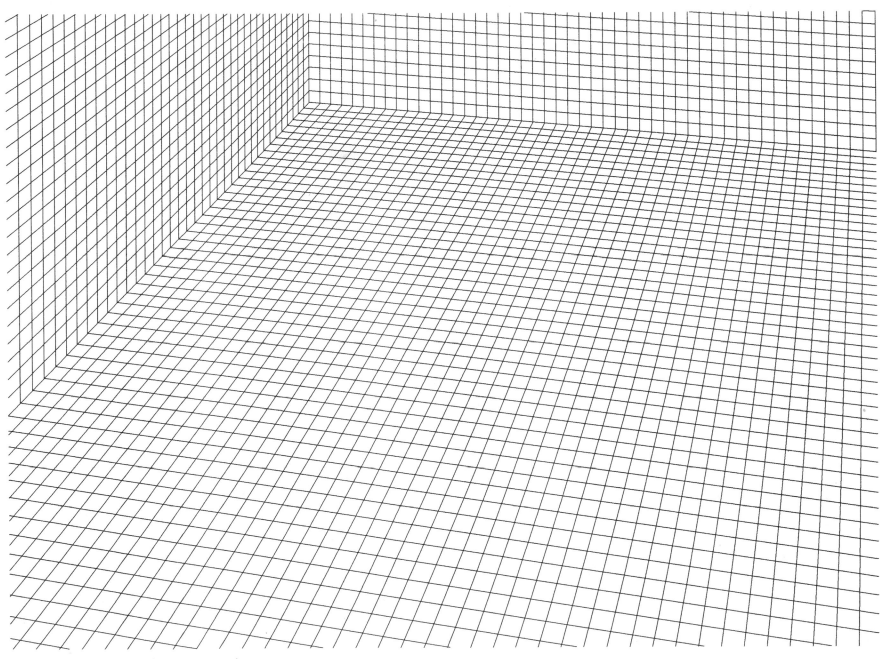

Bird's-eye view example 1, view 7, horizon line 100.

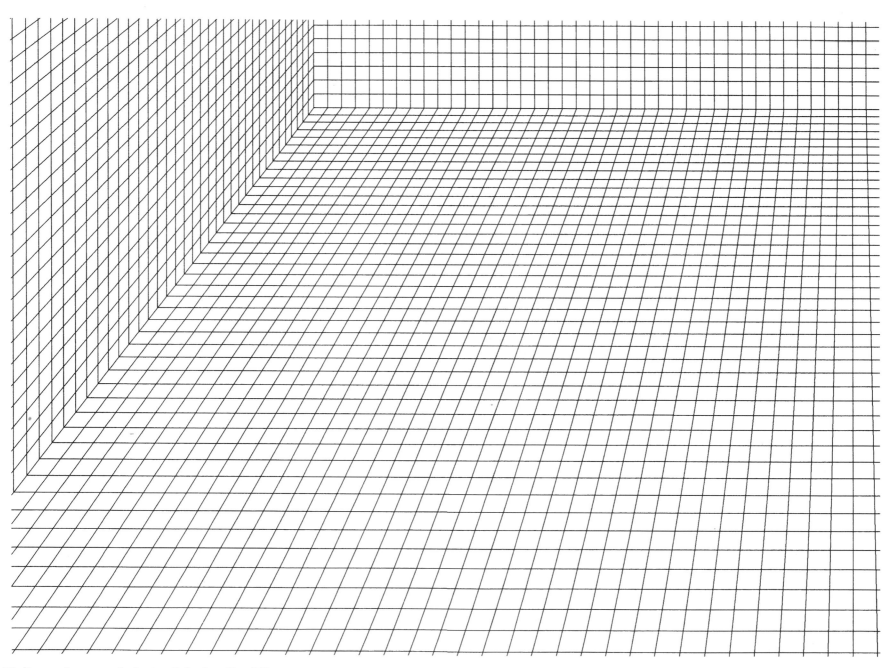

Bird's-eye view example 1, view 8, horizon line 100.

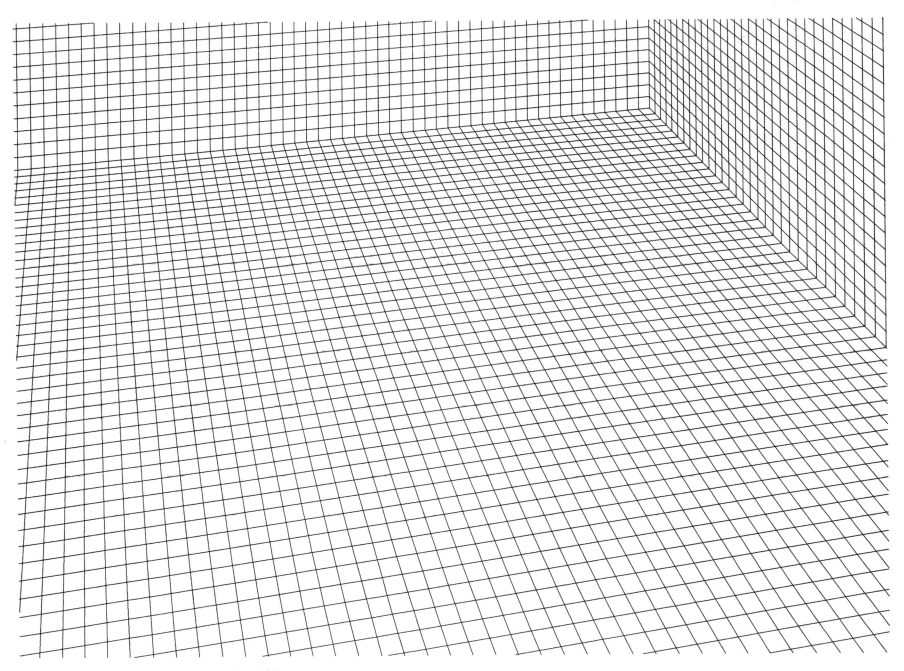

Bird's-eye view example 1, view 9, horizon line 100.

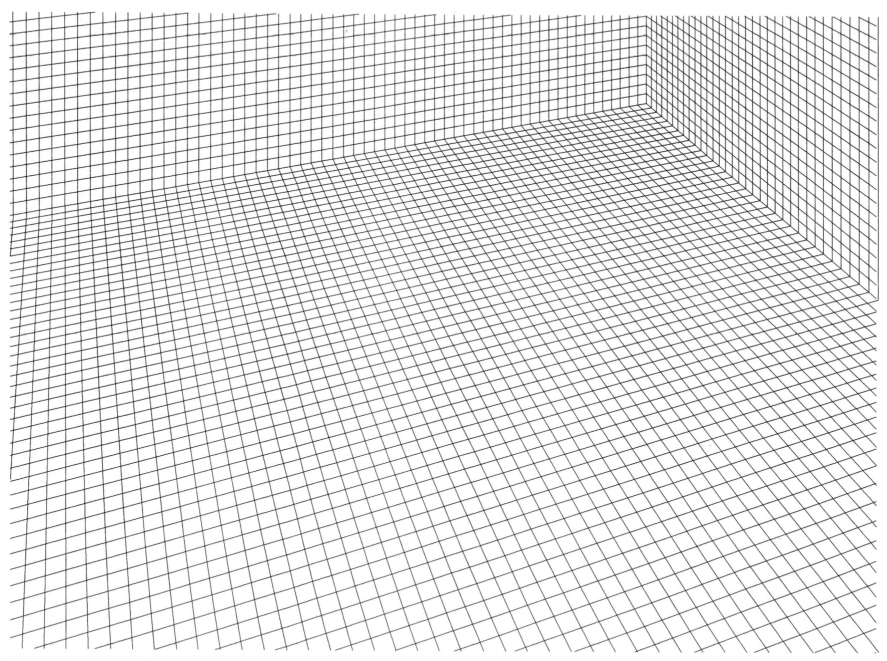

Bird's-eye view example 1, view 10, horizon line 100.

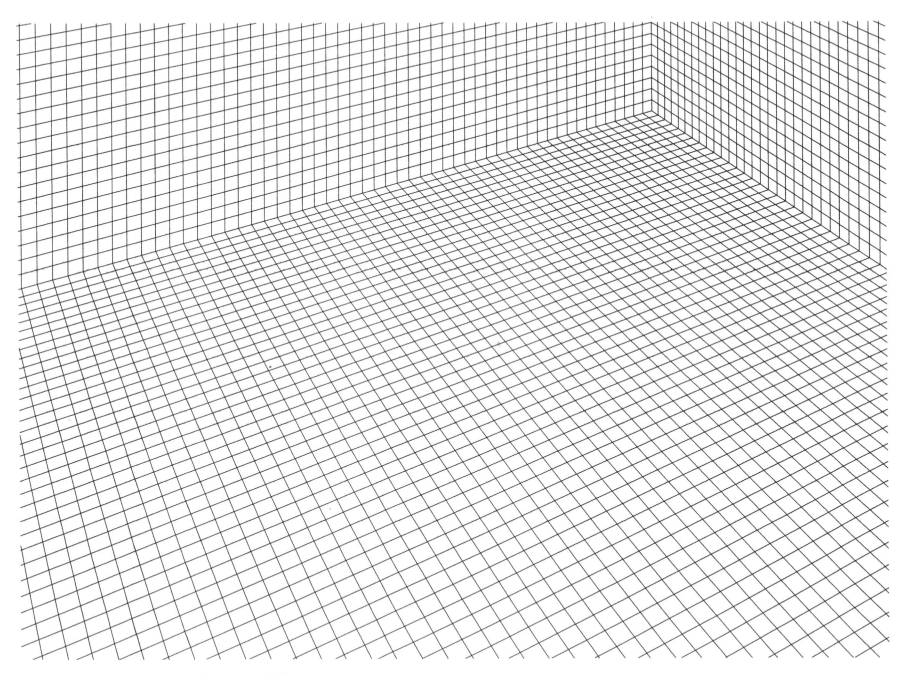

Bird's-eye view example 1, view 11, horizon line 100.

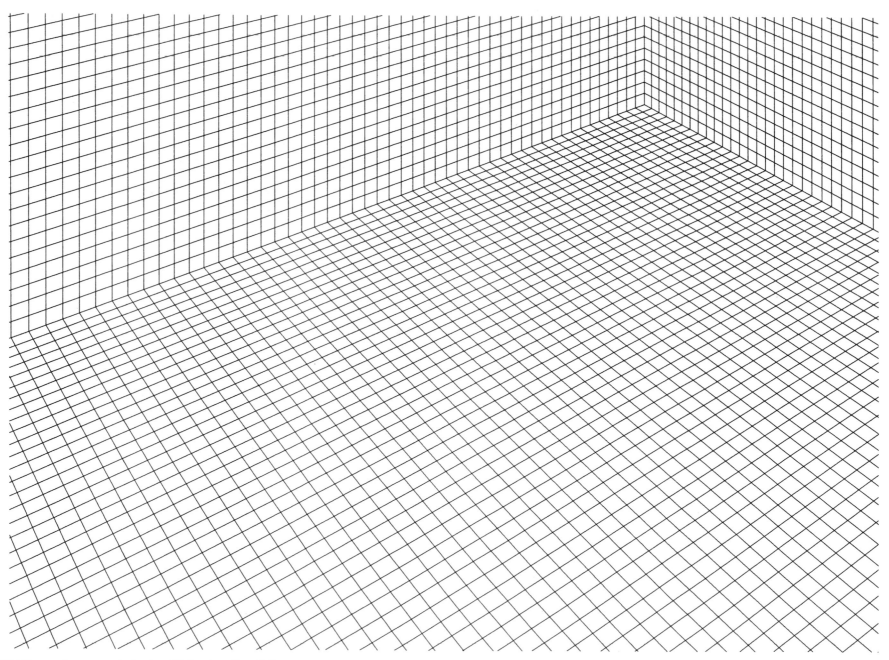

Bird's-eye view example 1, view 12, horizon line 100.

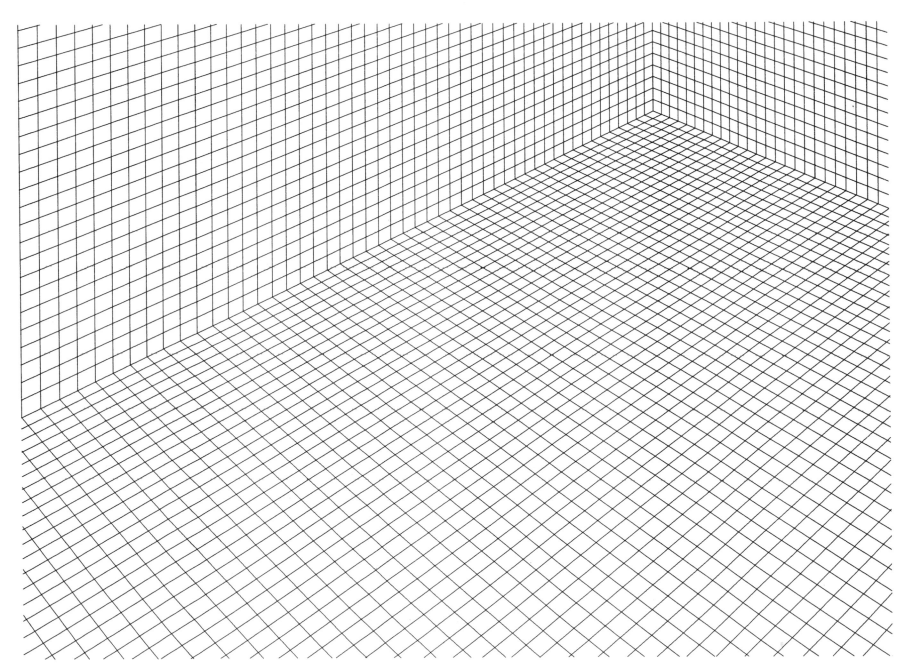

Bird's-eye view example 1, view 13, horizon line 100.

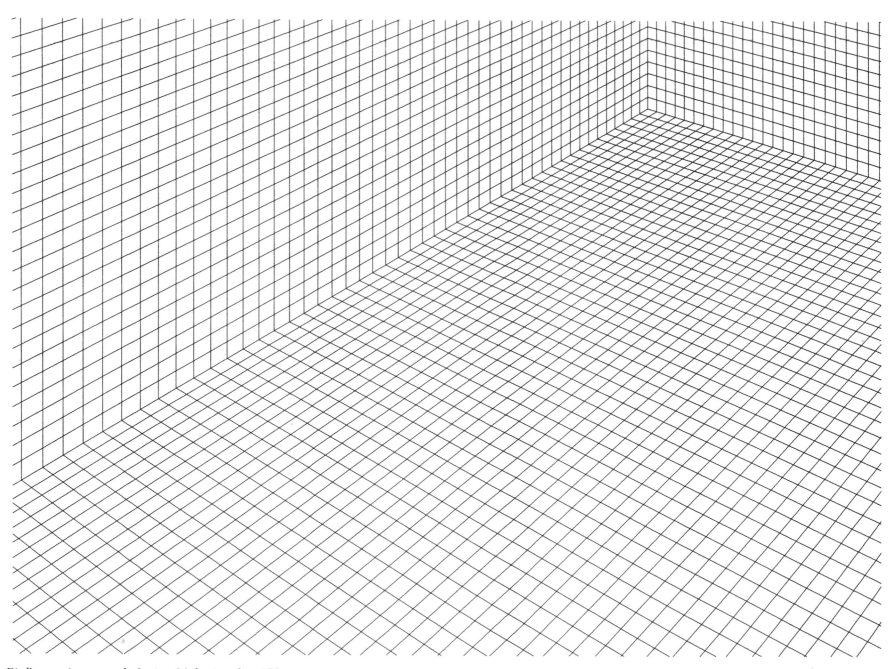

Bird's-eye view example 1, view 14, horizon line 100.

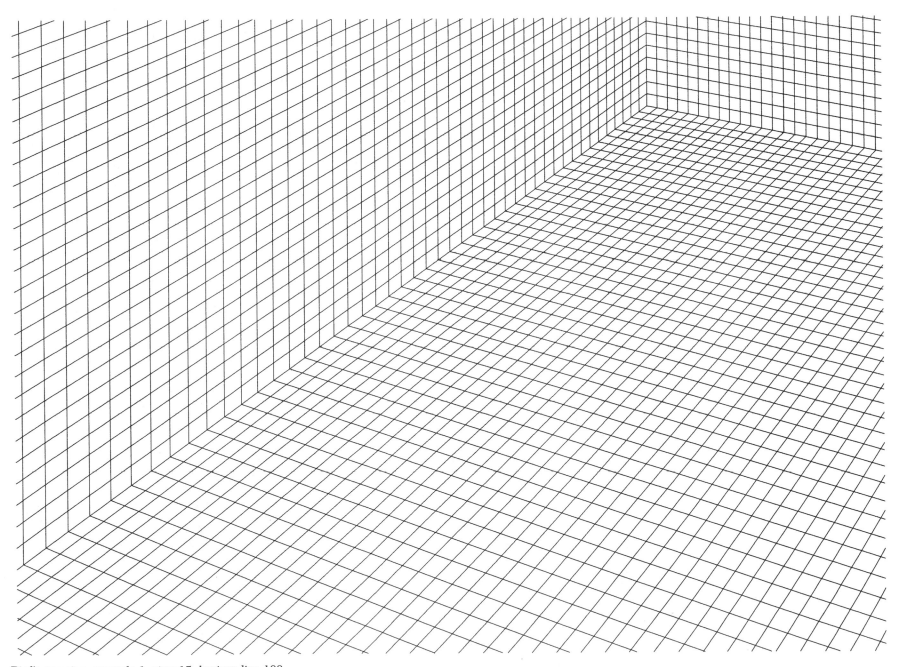

Bird's-eye view example 1, view 15, horizon line 100.

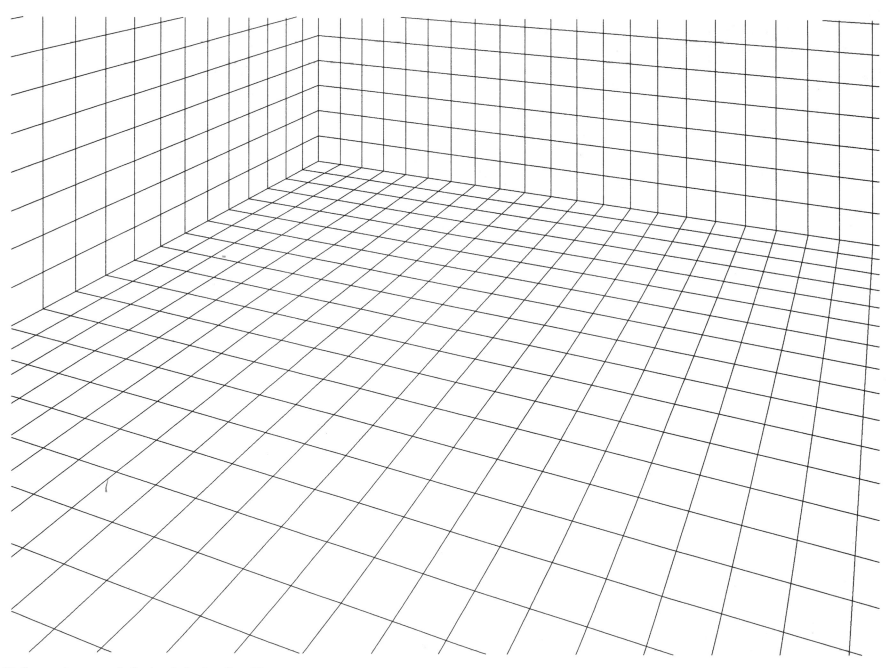

Bird's-eye view example 2, view 1, horizon line 20.

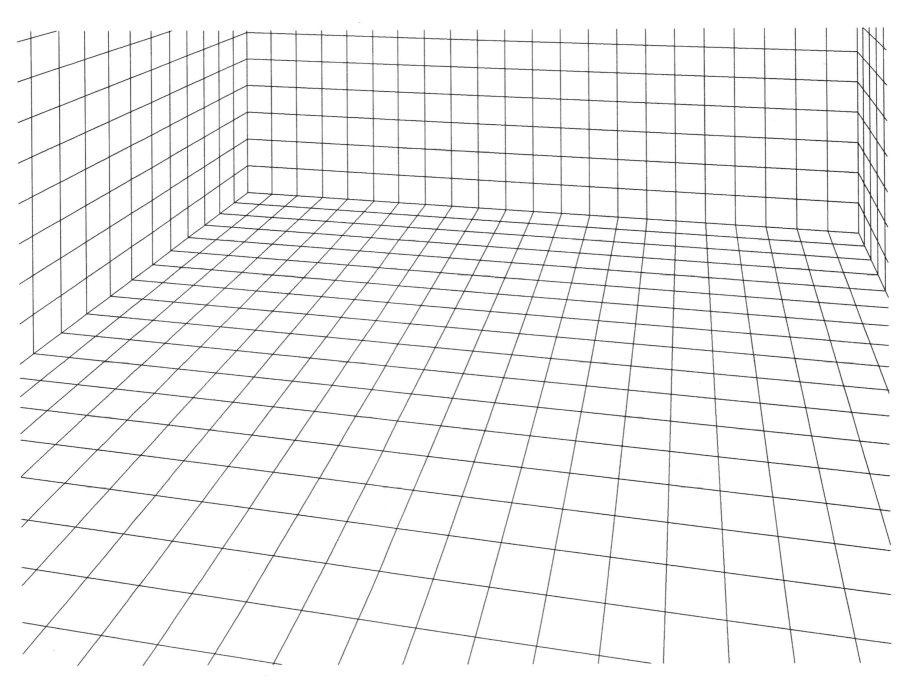

Bird's-eye view example 2, view 2, horizon line 20.

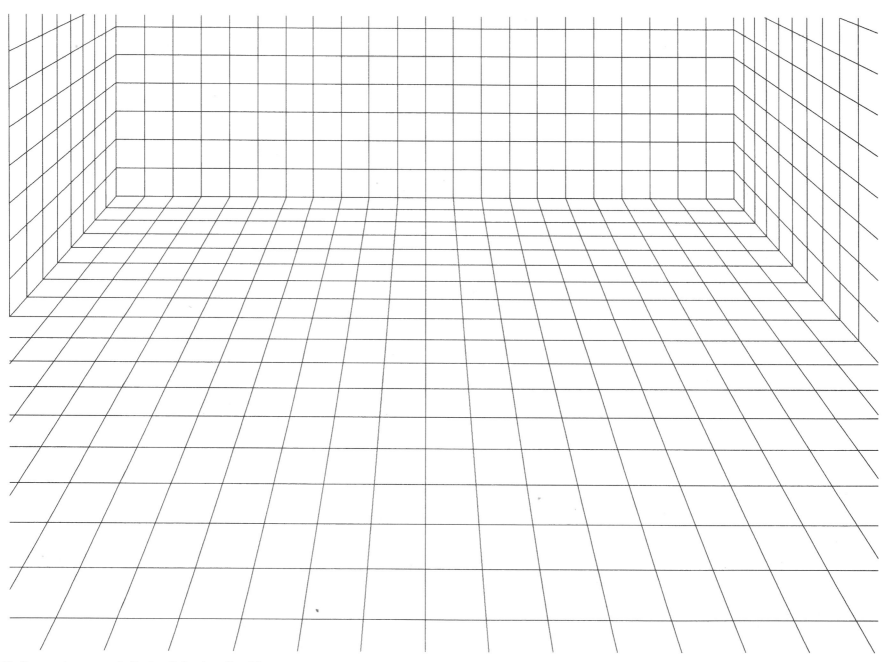

Bird's-eye view example 2, view 3, horizon line 20.

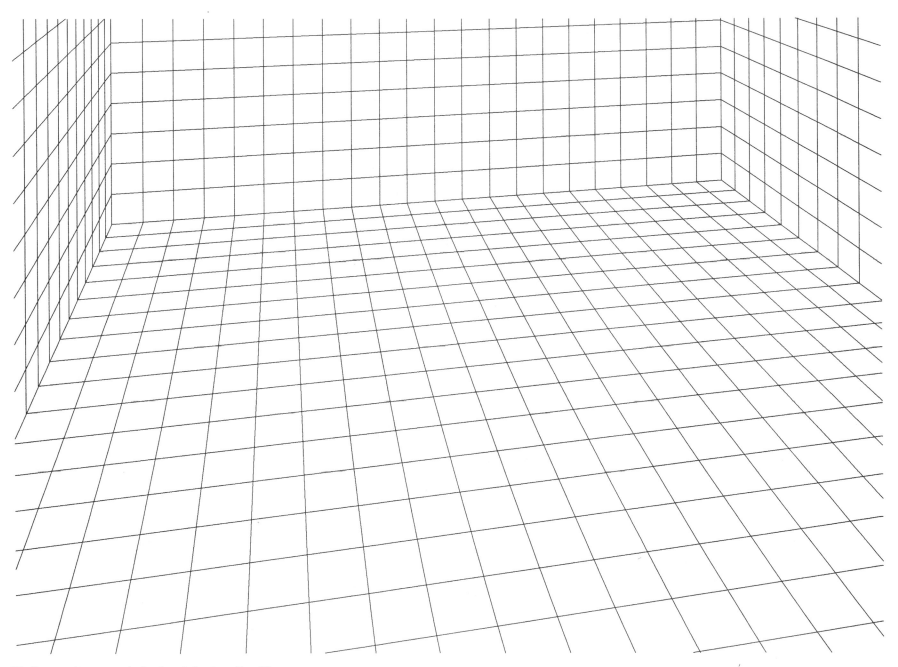

Bird's-eye view example 2, view 4, horizon line 20.

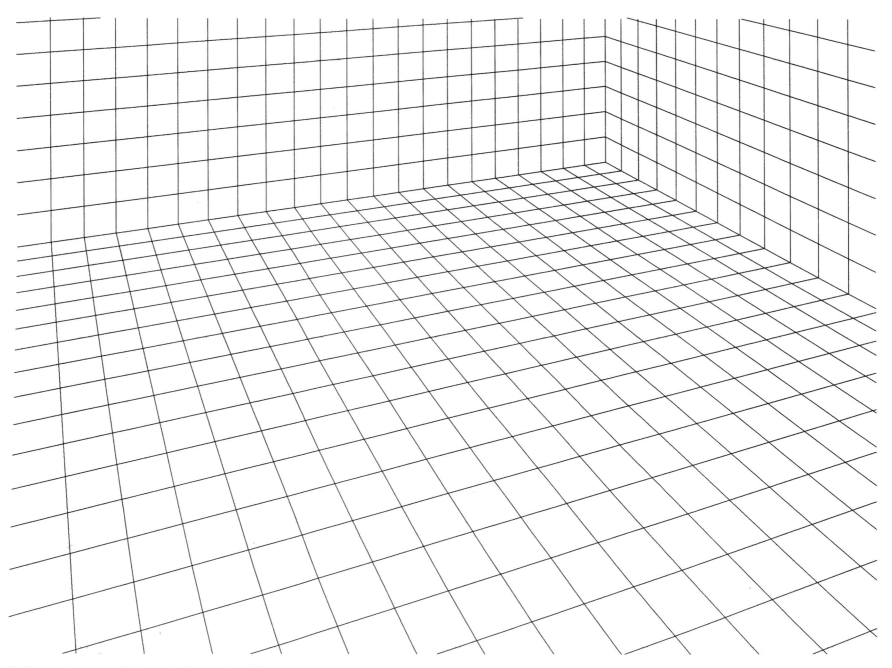

Bird's-eye view example 2, view 5, horizon line 20.

Perspective Grids for Exterior Design and Presentation

Not too long ago, we were working on a perspective for a sizable overseas project. By the time we finished, the client discovered that the mullions of the stair tower window on the east elevation did not match the mullions of the punched windows on the north elevation; and, the construction drawings were 100 percent completed. This happened because the design was done in two dimensions, not three. The elevations were done one by one, probably not by the same person. This reminds us of the importance of three-dimensional design. Using the perspective grids for exterior design, one could see more than one elevation at a time, so this kind of mistake could be easily avoided.

Example 1 uses an exterior grid to design a multistory office building in Washington, D.C. The project is to renovate the two existing Potomac Buildings in the Chinatown area owned by the District of Columbia government. These two buildings were undergoing a facelift, and the elevation studies were done for Turner Associates of Washington, D.C. One building faces H Street, and the other faces F Street; to make it simple, we show only the H Street building as an example. The planning commission required three different schemes for these buildings—one aluminum, one brick, and one concrete scheme; and since it is in Chinatown, it must also resemble Chinese architecture, at least in the lower levels. The renovation is basically for the skin of the building, and the floor plan will not undergo many changes. Therefore we can pick a grid without a floor measuring plane.

The H Street building is 75'0" wide, 200'0" long, and 113'0" high (not including the mechanical room); the first floor is 15'0" high, and the typical floors have a 10'0" floor-to-floor height. Let's assign 10'0" to each increment and indicate the 10'0", 20'0", 30'0",… marks along the X, Y, and Z axes. Then we can easily draw the configuration of the building and use our skill to design the details of the exterior of the building in aluminum (Fig. 3-1), brick (Fig. 3-2), and concrete (Fig. 3-3). The strip windows, which are about 6'0" high, are three-fifths of an increment; and the wall band, which is 4'0" high, is two-fifths of an increment. Using the same method, we can also plot the entrance, sidewalk, surrounding buildings, and all the entourage.

In this example, the overall dimensions of the building and the scale of the entourage are quite accurate, and according to the dimension marks on the grids we can estimate the size of any architectural detail on the drawings. Here we can also see the advantage of three-dimensional design: By using the exterior grid, we are designing two elevations at the same time, and the relationship of the windows, wall bands, etc., is clearly stated. So there is no way we can make the kind of mistakes that we mentioned previously.

The perspective grids not only are good for elevation design but also are ideal for constructing exterior perspectives from floor plans, elevations, and sections. In manual perspective construction, because of the restriction of the drafting board, sometimes the vanishing points are rather close together. Some students even put their vanishing points within the boundary of their paper. This means that the distance between the station point and the picture plane is very close. So the constructed perspective will look very distorted, much like a picture taken with an extrawide angle lens at a close distance. By using the computer-generated grids, we can locate the vanishing points at any distance along the horizon line without worrying whether the ruler is long enough or the drafting board big enough. Therefore the computer-generated grids can be drawn at any angle; they look either moderate or very dramatic.

Figure 3-1

Figure 3-2

Figure 3-3

Figure 3-4 shows a set of drawings of a commercial building ready for perspective construction. The user is asked to construct an eye-level perspective looking from an observer standing on the ground level at a certain distance to the picture plane. Figure 3-5 is a grid system chosen to construct this exterior perspective. This grid system is a two-point exterior perspective grid; it has two vertical measuring planes and a floor measuring plane. The floor measuring plane is extremely useful when the floor plan is an irregular shape. As we mentioned earlier, each increment of the grid lacks scale; the user must assign a scale to each increment. In this case we assigned 4'0" to each increment.

Now the perspective is seen by the observer standing on ground level, and the distance from the observer's feet to eye level is somewhere between 5'0" and 6'0". To make the perspective easier, we made it 6'0". Measure 6'0", which is one-half increment below the horizon line (HL); draw two dotted lines following the tapered lines on both sides of AF. This will determine the ground lines of the building. If you draw the building directly from the bottom lines of the vertical measuring planes, then the observer is looking at the building from a 12'0"-high level, and the perspective will not be an eye-level perspective. We identify the necessary dimensional marks on the floor and vertical measuring planes. Then we can plot the roof plan on the floor measuring planes with the dotted lines showing the recessed entrance.

In Fig. 3-6 we start to project vertical lines from the floor plan to mark the edges of the building, and we draw everything we can on the two vertical measuring planes. We can mark all horizontal wall bands at 4'0" and strip windows at 6'0" on the two vertical measuring planes, ADEF and ABGF. The mullions on the strip windows are 5'0" apart. We can use 5 increments, which is 20'0"; find the midpoint, which is 10'0"; and then find the midpoint of 10'0", which is 5'0". Figure 3-7 shows how the stepped corners at the left side of the building are constructed. Here we can project all vertical lines from the left corner of the floor measuring plane, where building planes change directions, indicating all the vertical "hinges" of the stepped corners. Here the word *hinge* means the intersec-tion line where the vertical planes change direction. The tapered lines on both sides of a hinge follow the direction of the tapered lines on the two vertical measuring planes, by using a triangle as mentioned in Chap. 1. In this example we can see that the floor measuring plane is very useful to plot details that do not fall immediately on the vertical measuring planes.

Figure 3-8 shows the construction of the entrance which has two non-axial planes. These two nonaxial planes are shown on the floor measuring planes as lines SN and KT. To construct SN and KT, first we need to construct axial lines MN and KL. Then we can draw tapered lines KL and LM on the vertical measuring planes, using the method shown in Fig. 3-6. We project a vertical line from T on the floor measuring plane and that intersects LM at T on the vertical view, and we connect TK and TM in the same view. Thus we have drawn the nonaxial lines in perspective.

Figure 3-9 shows how a perspective can be drawn when it is running out of register with the perspective grid. In the construction of the mechanical room of this commercial project, this situation will appear. On the floor measuring plane, first extend WV and XU until they intersect AB at K and N. From K and N pump up vertical lines beyond the top of the vertical measuring plane. Plot approximately $3\frac{3}{4}$ increments, which equal 15'0", until they reach P and Q. Draw tapered lines from P and Q following the tapered lines on the vertical measuring plane (ADEF) until they intersect the vertical lines pumped up from the floor plan of the mechanical room on the floor measuring plane. Thus we have completed the construction of the mechanical room. Figure 3-10 is the final result, showing the configuration of the exterior perspective with the grid system removed.

The 26 exterior grids that follow represent a cross-section of exterior views and angles that can be used to construct perspectives for low- to midrise projects. Some of the grids provided include the floor plane grid for help in constructing the perspective. A second set of grids includes the ground plan for the addition of entourage to your drawing. Additional grids can be accessed from the book's accompanying disk. See Chap. 6 for how to access these grids.

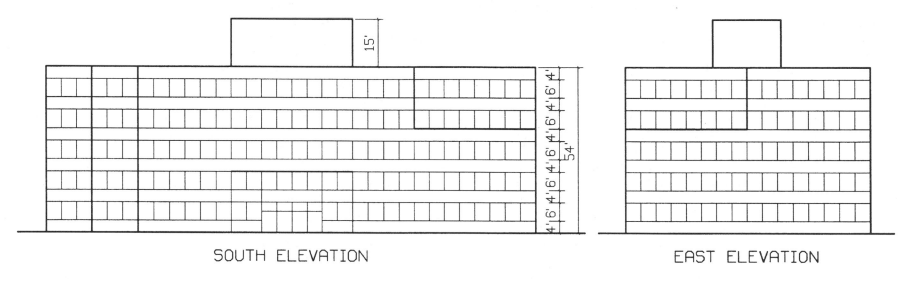

SOUTH ELEVATION

EAST ELEVATION

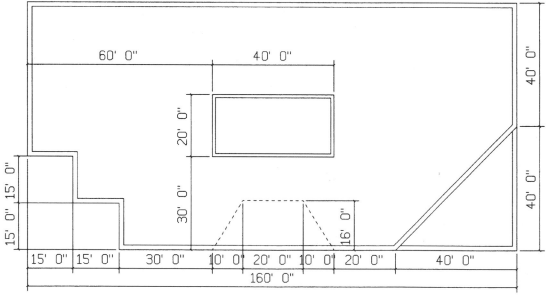

ROOF PLAN

Figure 3-4

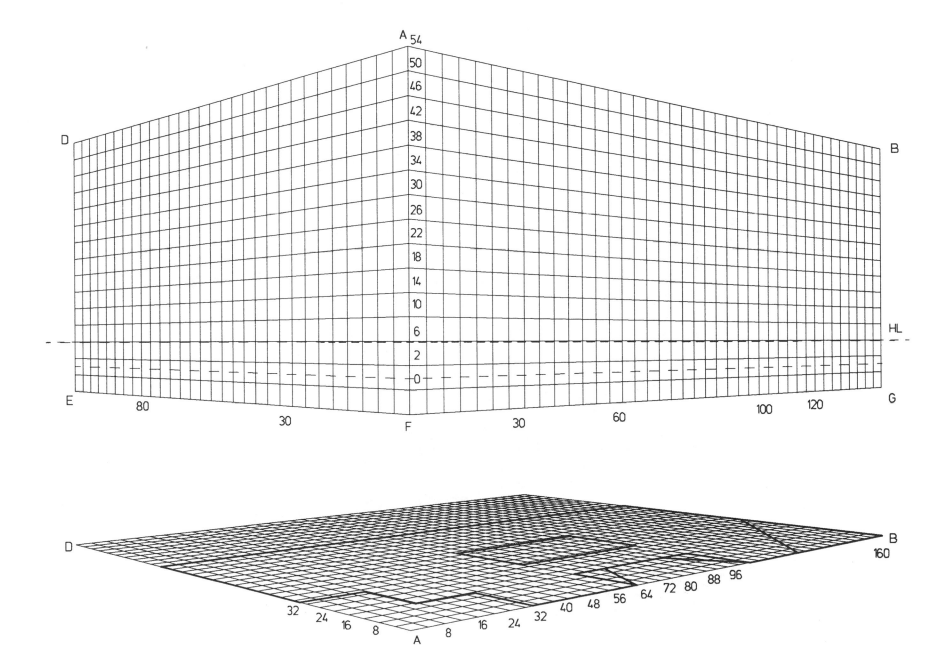

Figure 3-5

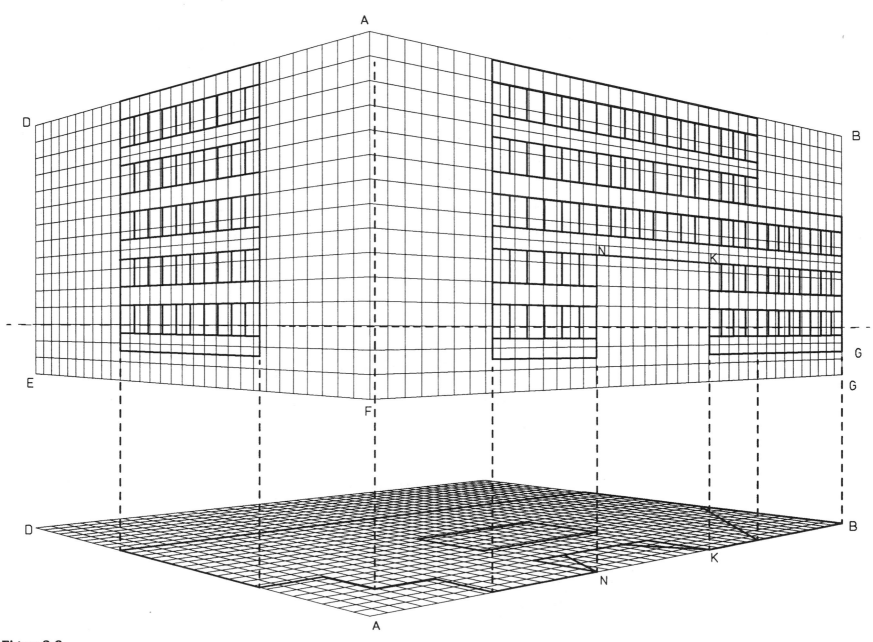

Figure 3-6

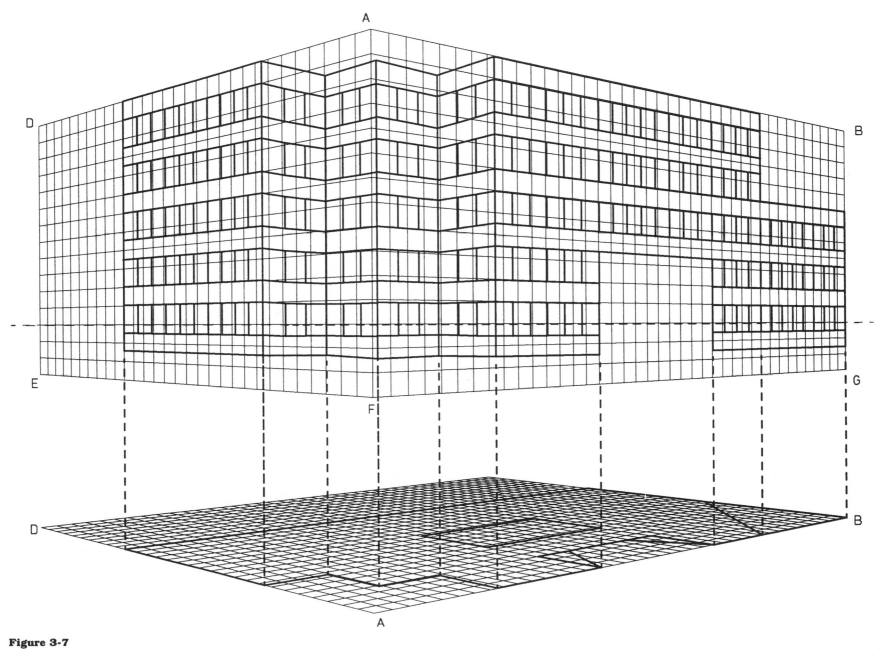

Figure 3-7

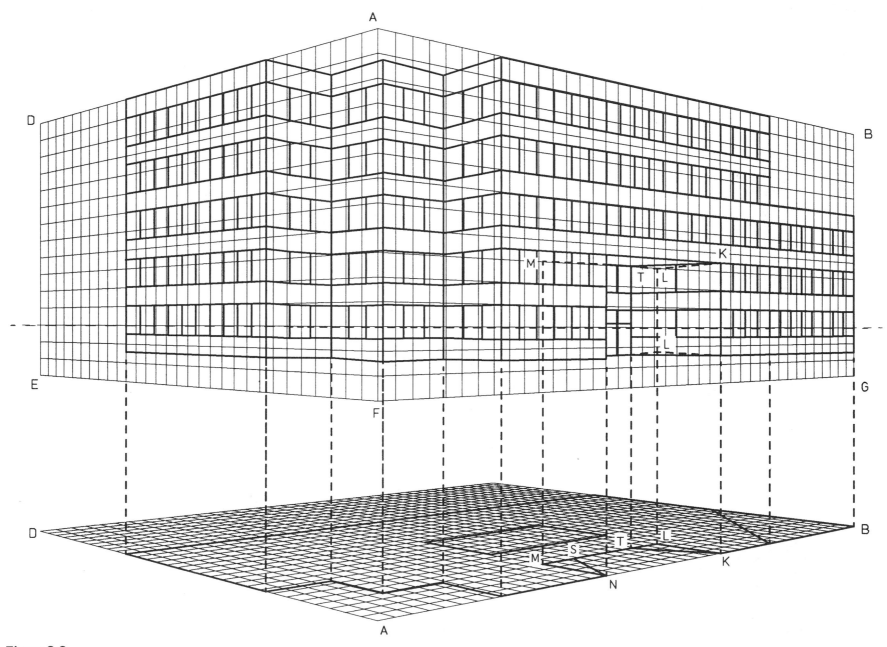

Figure 3-8

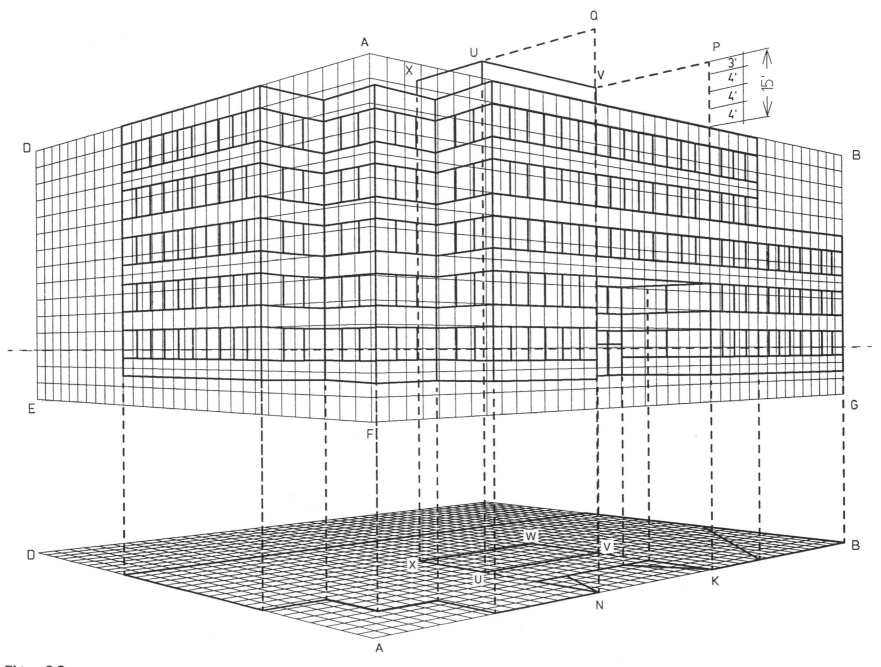

Figure 3-9

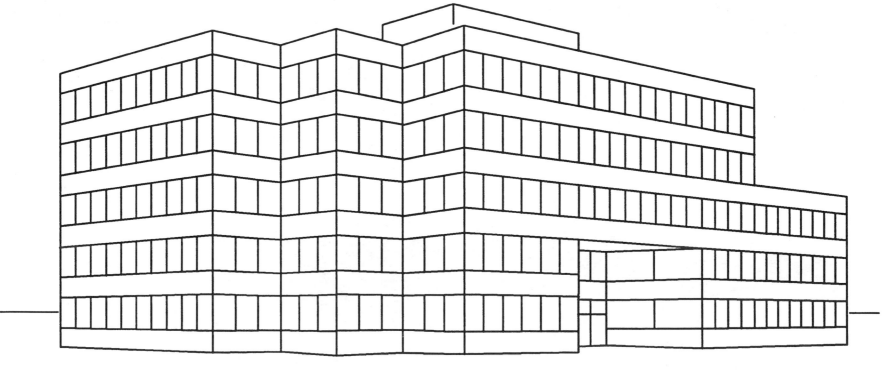

Figure 3-10

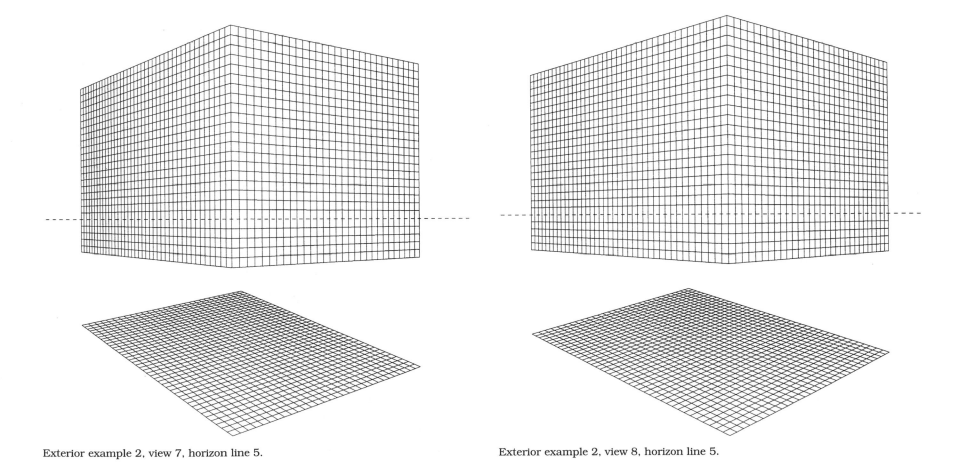

Exterior example 2, view 7, horizon line 5.

Exterior example 2, view 8, horizon line 5.

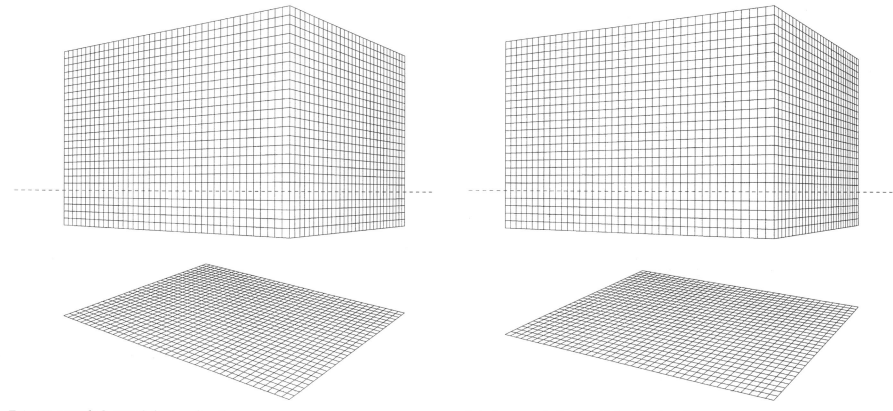

Exterior example 2, view 9, horizon line 5.

Exterior example 2, view 10, horizon line 5.

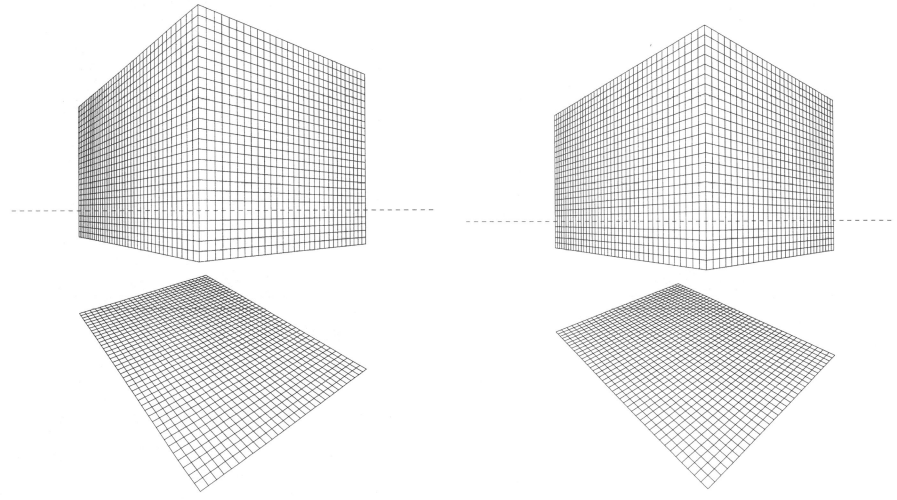

Exterior example 2, view 12, horizon line 5.   Exterior example 2, view 13, horizon line 5.

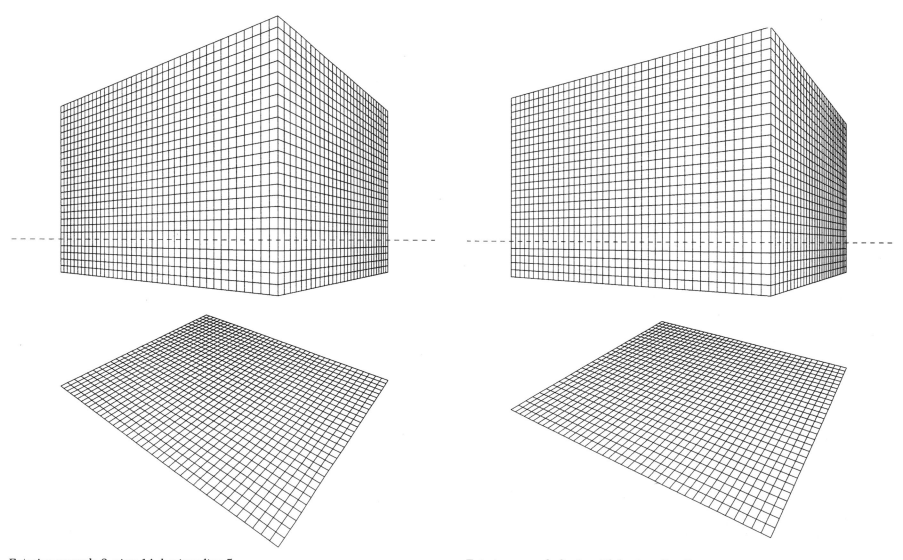

Exterior example 2, view 14, horizon line 5.

Exterior example 2, view 15, horizon line 5.

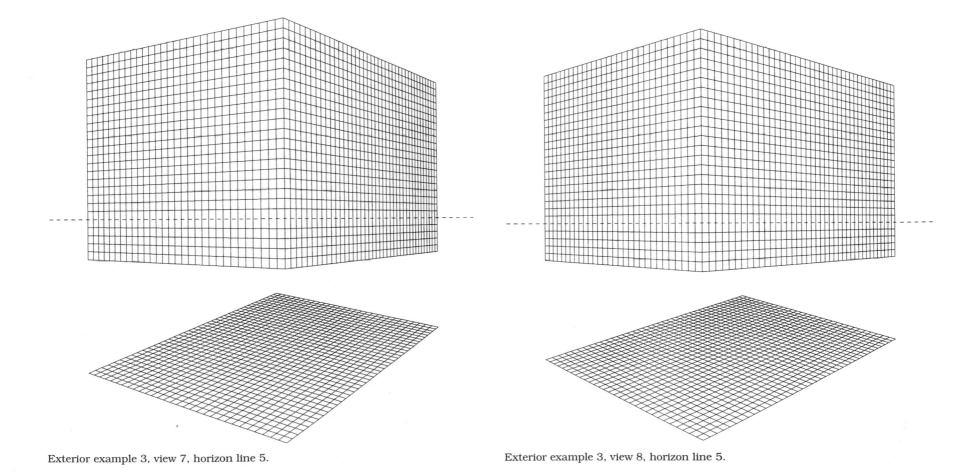

Exterior example 3, view 7, horizon line 5.

Exterior example 3, view 8, horizon line 5.

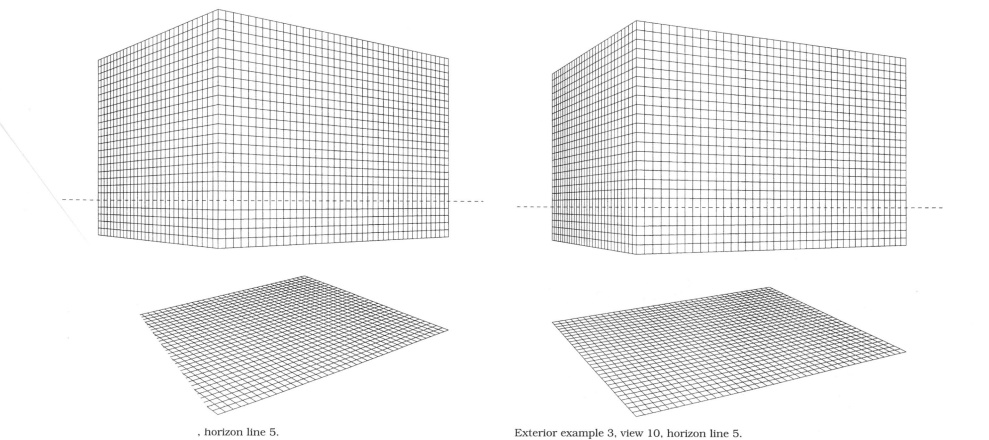

, horizon line 5.   Exterior example 3, view 10, horizon line 5.

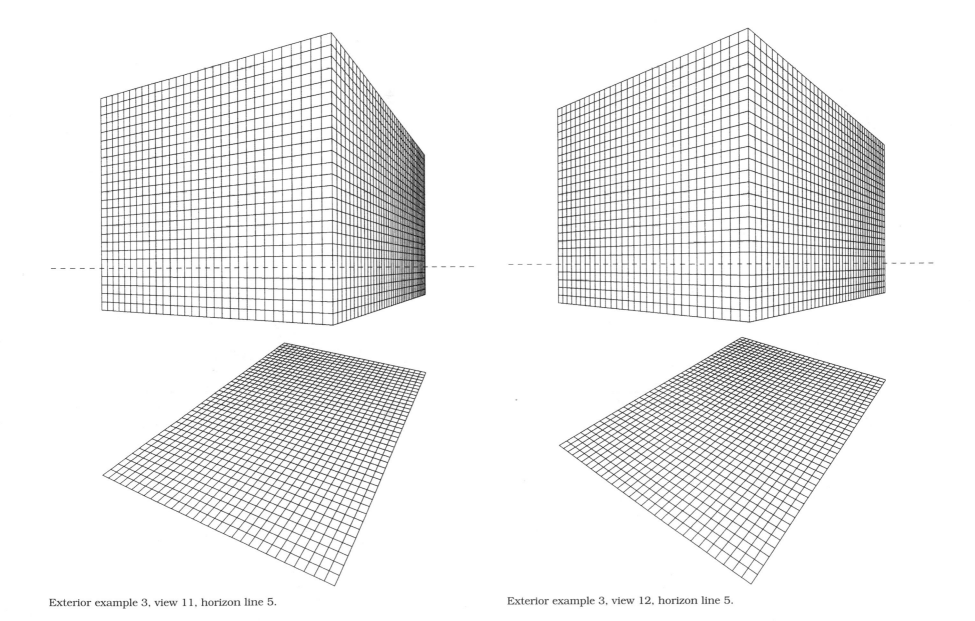

Exterior example 3, view 11, horizon line 5.

Exterior example 3, view 12, horizon line 5.

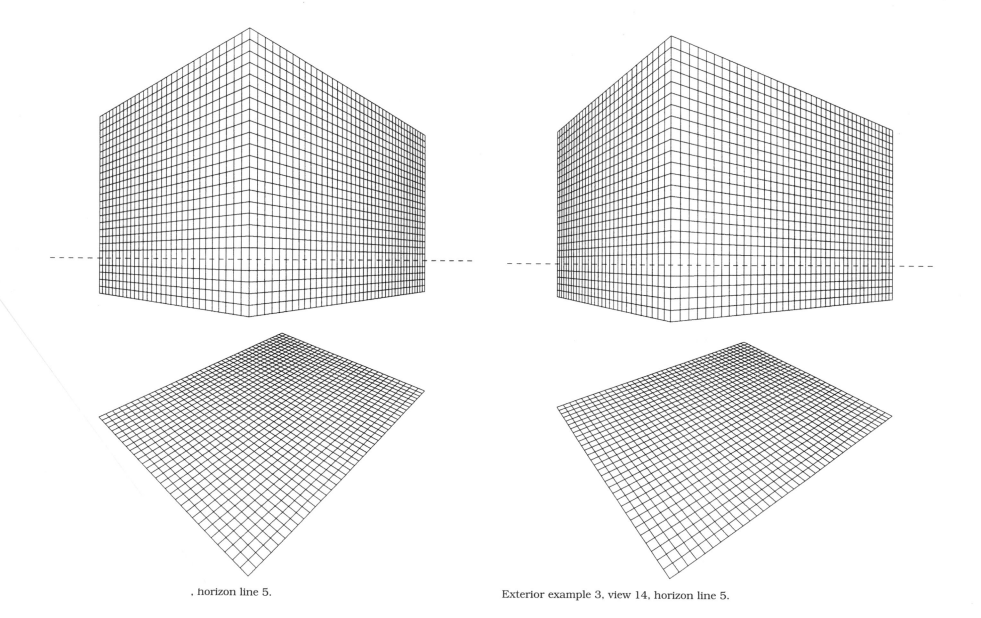

, horizon line 5.

Exterior example 3, view 14, horizon line 5.

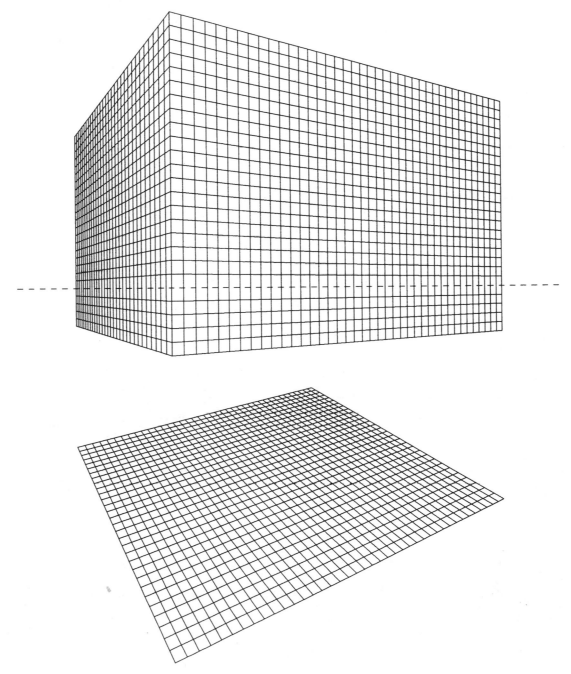

Exterior example 3, view 15, horizon line 5.

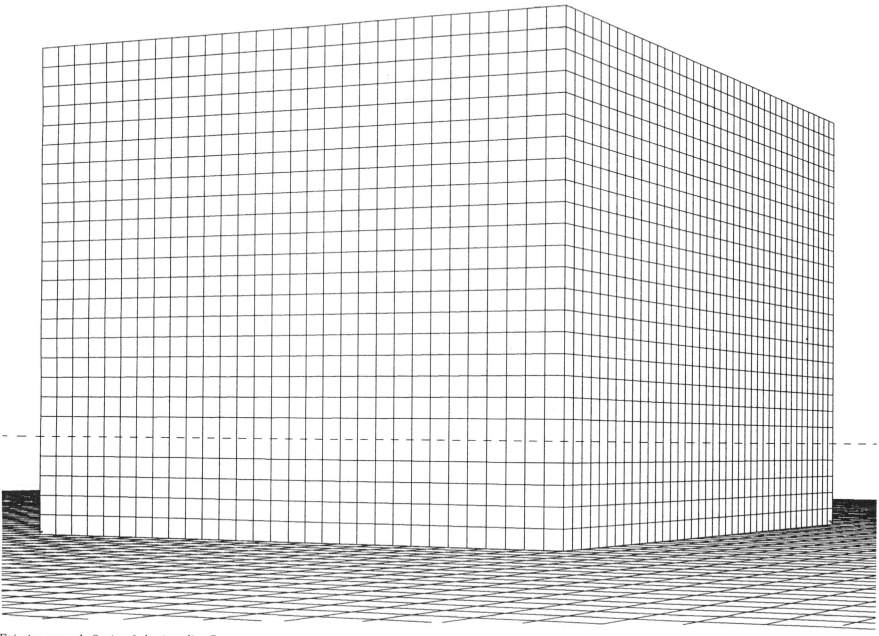

Exterior example 6, view 1, horizon line 5.

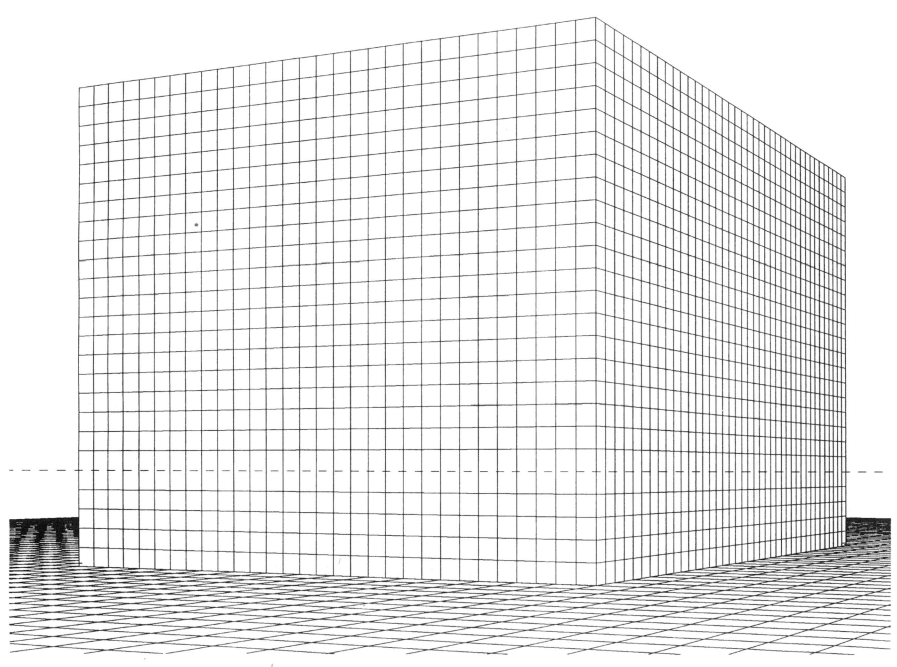

Exterior example 6, view 6, horizon line 5.

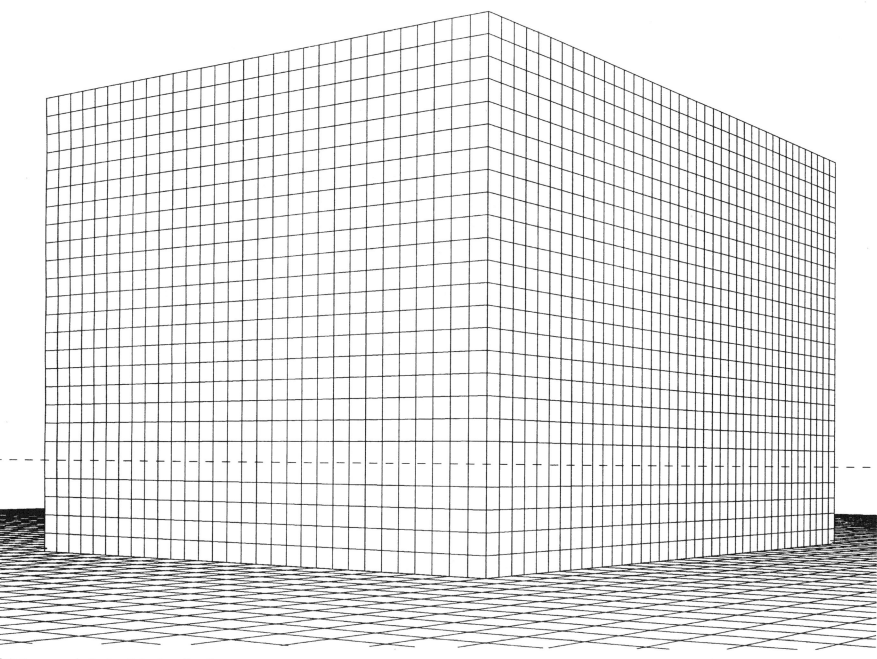

Exterior example 6, view 7, horizon line 5.

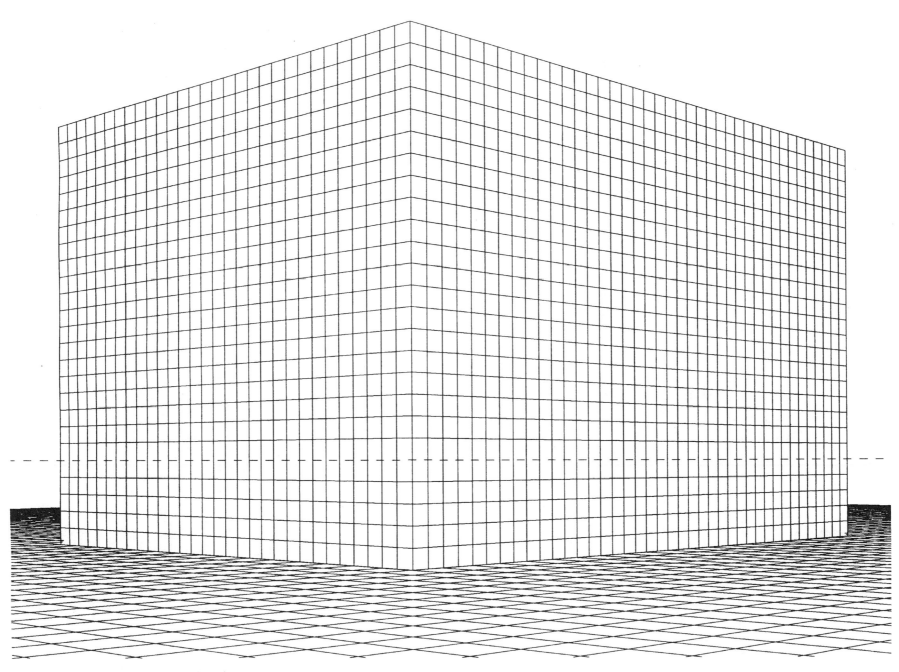

Exterior example 6, view 8, horizon line 5.

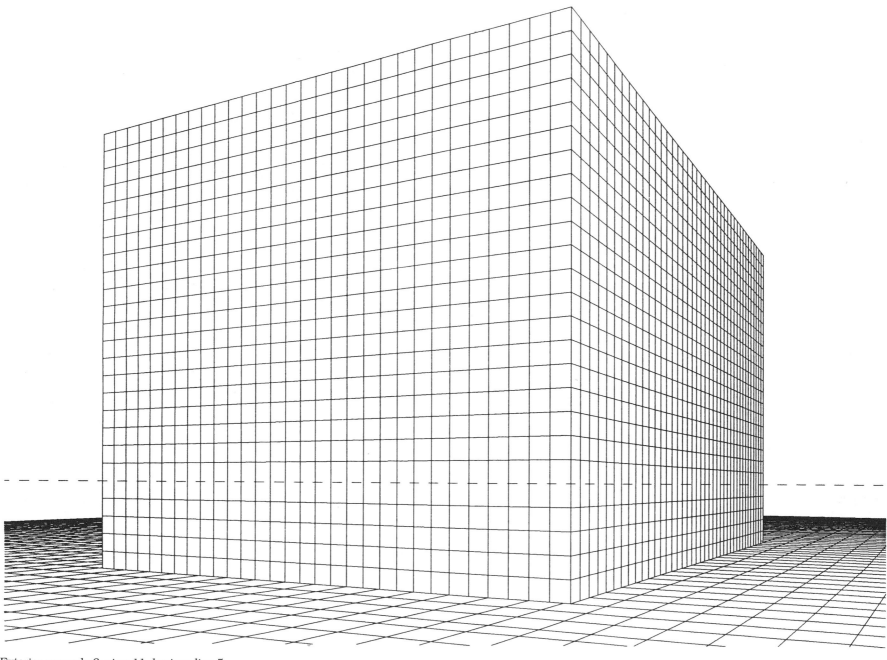

Exterior example 6, view 11, horizon line 5.

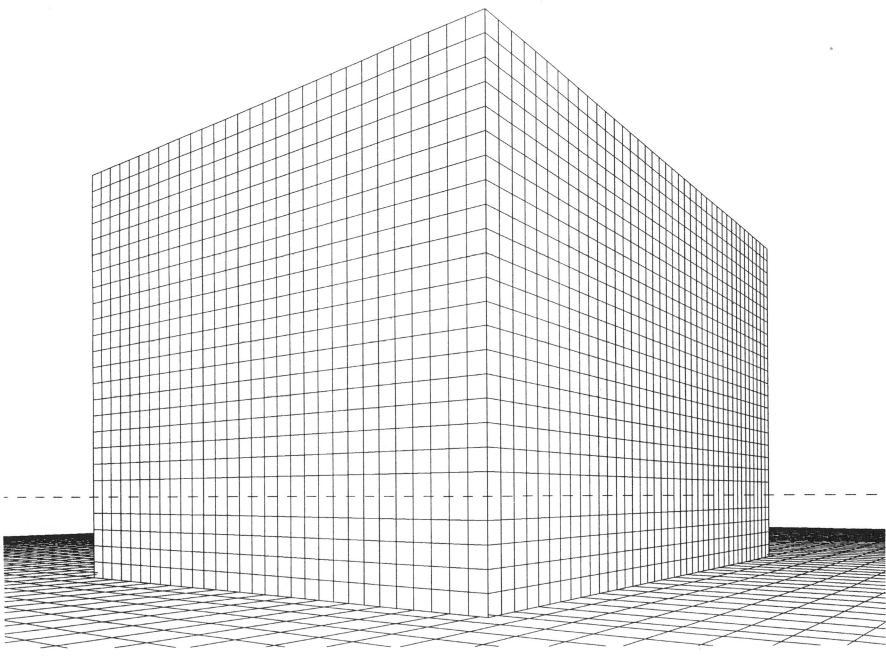

Exterior example 6, view 12, horizon line 5.

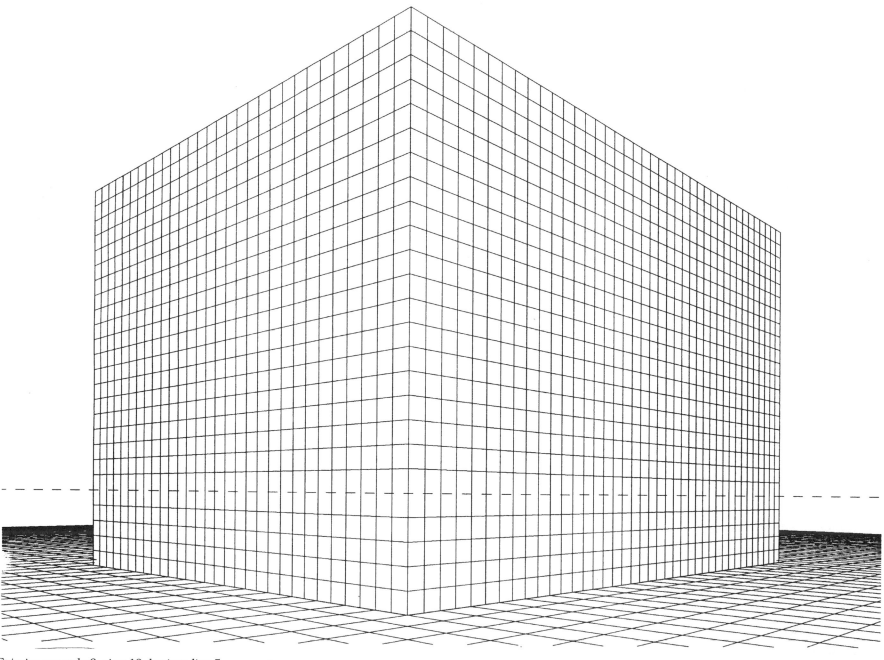

Exterior example 6, view 13, horizon line 5.

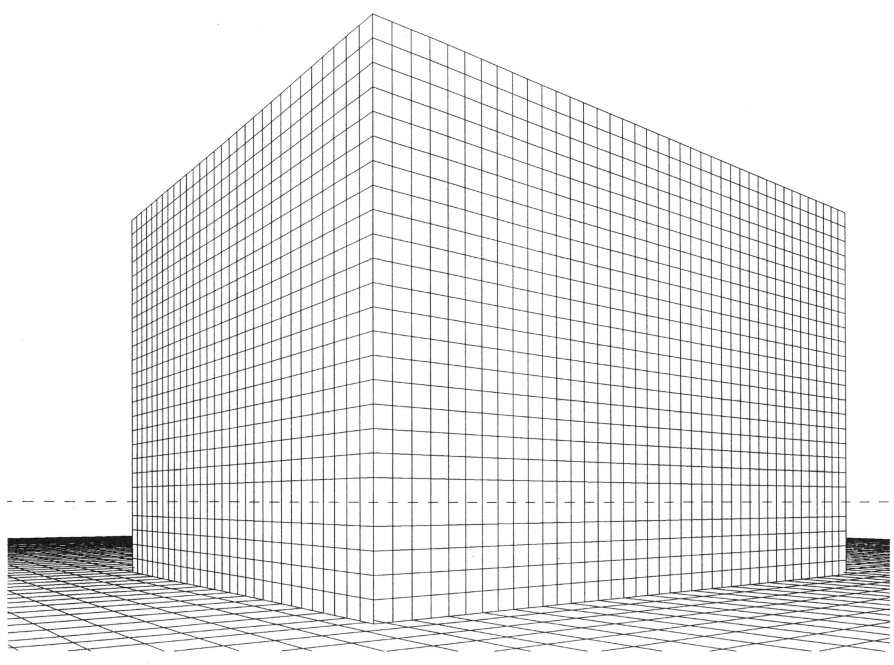

Exterior example 6, view 14, horizon line 5.

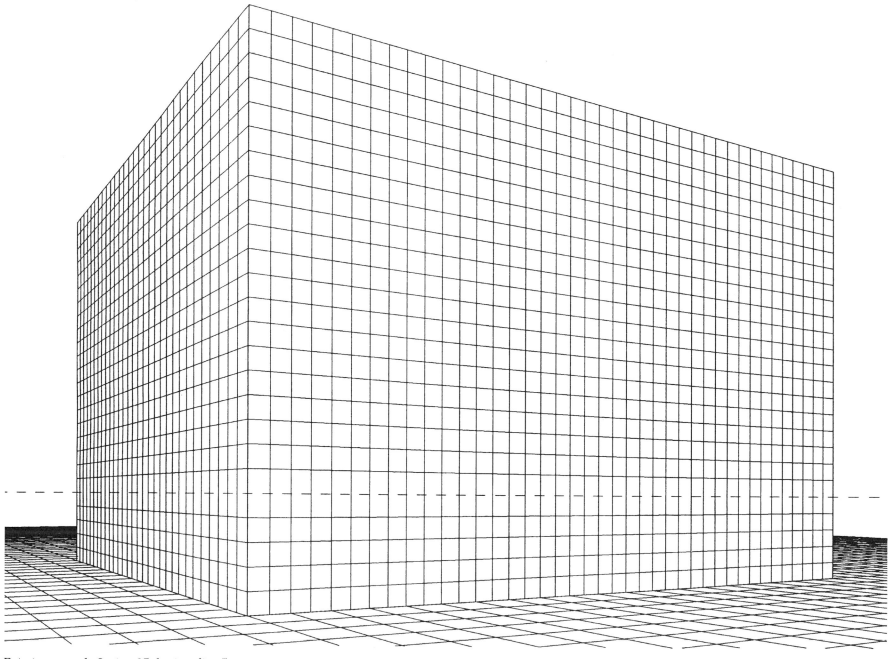

Exterior example 6, view 15, horizon line 5.

Perspective Grids for Interior Design and Presentation

The ancient Chinese philosopher Lao-tzu once said that when one drinks from a cup, the useful part of the cup is not the cup itself, but the negative space enclosed by the cup. Frank Lloyd Wright totally agreed with this philosophy and considered that the reality of architecture is not its walls or its ceiling, but the inhabitable space enclosed by these elements. In this respect the interior spatial design is crucial to the success of any building design.

The old method of interior design was to design six planes separately. These six planes were the floor plan, the reflected ceiling plan, and the four (or maybe more) interior elevations. One can hardly visualize how all six planes work together. By using the perspective grid for this purpose, not only can we design these plans and elevations simultaneously but also we can design the negative space enclosed by these elements.

Example 1 (Figs. 4-1 to 4-3) shows how we can do a three-dimensional design of an interior space even when we lack a floor plan, interior elevations, and sections. The project is a vacation house located in South Lake Tahoe, California. Here we are to design a room with a view. It is a living room with a dining enclave approximately 20′0″ by 26′0″ and 8′0″ high. Let's choose a grid that is most suitable for this purpose. Then we make each increment 1′0″, and the horizon line (the dotted line on the grid) is 5′0″. All five planes (floor measuring plane, ceiling measuring plane, and three vertical measuring planes) shown on this perspective grid are measurable. There is a view looking through the back wall, and there are no adjacent rooms to the left side of the room.

Our purpose here is to design as many openings to the lake as possible. We also want to increase the height of this room, so we decided to design a cathedral ceiling with a ridgeline 5′0″ above the 8′0″ height. In Fig. 4-1 first we find the center point (I) at the top of the back wall, extend

line IH to J, set IJ = IH = 5′0″, and connect JC and JK. We have drawn the gable wall adjacent to the cathedral ceiling. We extend any tapered line on the ceiling measuring plane to the back wall; when it intersects the horizon line, we have located the near vanishing point VP. Connecting J to this vanishing point and extending it beyond J, we have thus determined the ridgeline.

Assume that we want to design a deck 8′0″ from the back wall in order to experience the view from outside. We can use a method called *diagonals through the bisectors.* First pick a 4′0″ distance from the back wall to point A. Find the center of the intersection of the back wall and the left wall, which is 4′0″ above the floor. Draw a line from A through this point until it intersects the extension line of the intersection of the floor and the left wall at B. Draw a perpendicular line BE. Extend the centerline of the left wall until it crosses BE at F. Connect CF and extend it until it intersects that extension line again at D. To find the height of the railing, measure 3′ on the left wall from the floor and extend it until it intersects perpendicular line DG at D. Draw horizontal tapered lines following this 3′ mark, and the drawing of the railing and the deck outside the room is complete.

We can see from this example that if the perspective is running out of register, we can always add or subtract to what fits the design purpose.

In Fig. 4-2 we are to open as many windows to the view as possible. Since all these windows are located on the three vertical measuring planes, we just plot them directly on these measuring planes according to the dimensions we prefer. We can design a corner window 4′0″ by 5′0″ and 3′0″ from the floor. Then there are four 3′6″ by 5′0″ windows and a 6′0″ by 8′0″ patio door on the back wall as well as another 4′0″ window on the left wall. We can also design a polygon-shaped window on the gable wall.

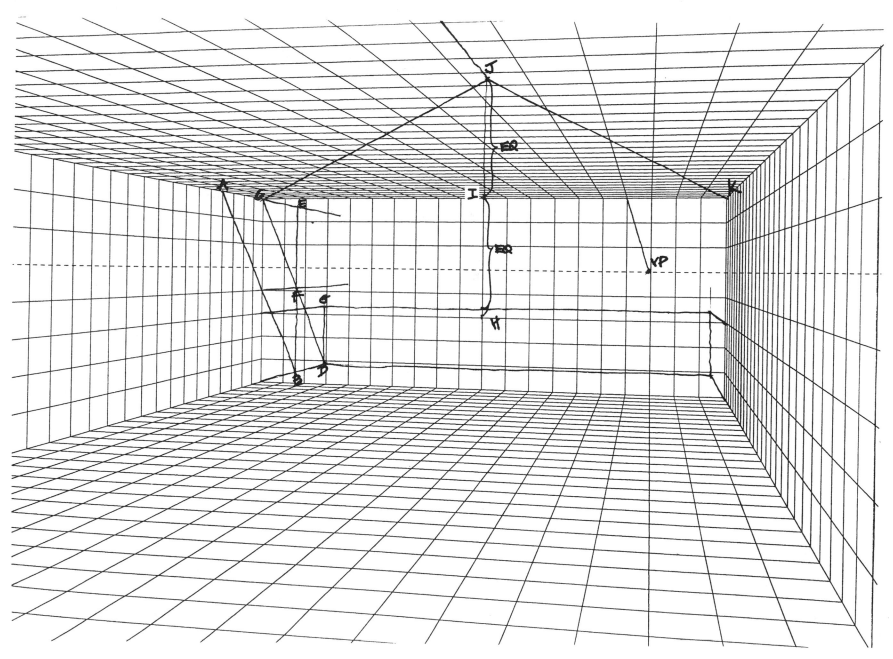

Figure 4-1

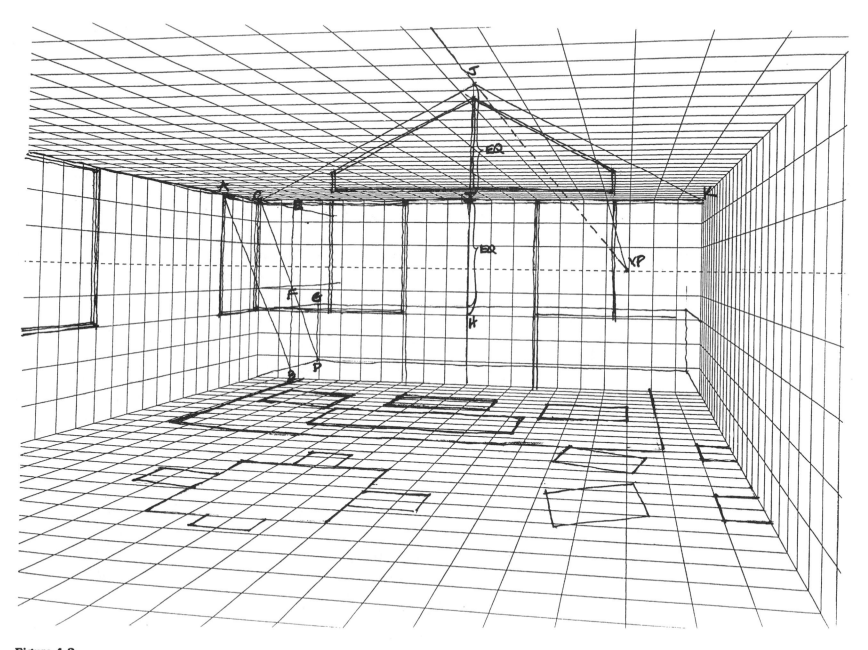

Figure 4-2

In Fig. 4-2 we start to locate some furnishings for the room, by first drawing their footprints on the floor measuring plane. Since there is a view, it is reasonable to have a sofa set grouping facing that view. We start to lay out the footprints of a sofa set with a coffee table and an area rug. Near the left wall we laid out a dining table grouping, and on the right wall we designed a fireplace. We drew in the footprint of the fireplace and the two chairs facing the fireplace.

Figure 4-3 shows how we can complete the design by pumping up the heights of all the elements in this space, changing two-dimensional images to three-dimensional images. First we construct the fireplace on the right wall and project the back lines of the fireplace until they intersect the right vertical measuring plane and the ceiling measuring plane. The upper part of the fireplace is sloped because of the cathedral roof. To find that slope, we measure 1'0" from K to U, and from U we extend a vertical line until it crosses the top of the gable line at L. Connect the line from near vanishing point VP to L and extend it until it crosses the two vertical lines projected from the fireplace footprint at M and N. Assume the fireplace opening is 4'0" wide and 3'6" high. Measure P which is at 3'6". We draw a horizontal tapered line, cross the vertical line at Q, connect this point to VP; thus we can determine the height of the fireplace opening.

Next we pump up all the furniture pieces to their required heights. We are using the three vertical measuring planes to do our measurements. Since all the pieces of furniture in this space are away from the three vertical measuring planes, we have to construct their heights by relating them to the heights on these planes. For instance, we want to give a height to the table, which is 2'6". We extend the back line RS of the table footprint until it touches the bottom of the wall at W, measure up 2'6", and draw a tapered line back until it touches the two vertical lines projected from R and S at V and T.

To avoid too many overlaps, we draw first the furniture items in front of the perspective, then the ones behind.

After we have drawn all the furniture, we can use a heavier marker and darken some of the lines to make the drawing stand out more. We add some landscape that we see through the glass area. We also add a wall base and some texture to the area carpet.

Because it is a sketch, if we have made some mistakes somewhere, we just leave them there and draw the correct ones right next to them.

Now we have completed a three-dimensional design of an interior space. Since all the walls, floor, and ceiling are drawn on a grid system, it is not hard to translate them to two-dimensional floor plan, interior elevations, and sections if we feel the need.

Example 2 constructs an interior perspective from existing floor plans, elevations, and sections (Figs. 4-4 to 4-8). This example shows the interior lobby space of a commercial building. The lobby is 40'0" by 40'0" and 20'0" high with a mezzanine in between. The information provided is simply for the purpose of constructing the perspective.

Figures 4-9 to 4-11 show the step-by-step construction of this interior perspective. In Fig. 4-9 we use the same grid as in the previous example. We just flip it upside down and let each increment represent 2'0" to fit our purpose. In this situation, the horizon line is at 6'0" level. Extend any line that vanishes to the back. It will intersect the horizon line, and we can determine the near vanishing point VP. Here the height of the back wall is 20'0", and the height of the grid is 16'0". Again it is running out of register. We need not worry, for we can always adjust the grids to our needs. In this case we have to add 4'0". On the back wall AB is 4'0". Extend AB to C and make BC = AB. We now have our 20'0" height. From C we draw a tapered line following the tapered lines on the ceiling measuring plane until it intersects the extended vertical line on the left at D. From C and D we connect lines following the tapered lines that vanish to VP, and we have constructed a new box to fit our actual situation.

In Fig. 4-10 we start to construct the balcony by measuring 10 increments, which is 20'0" from the back wall. To determine the height and configuration, we simply use the measurements on the left or right measuring planes. To locate the three little pickets, find their location on the floor measuring plane and project them up vertically. The two elevator doors and one exit door are all on the back wall, so we can draw them out directly on this rear vertical measuring plane.

To draw the columns, first we locate their footprints on the floor measuring plane and project vertical lines up from the footprints. To find the location of the top of the column under the balcony, we measure three increments which are 6'0" from the fascia of the balcony to E, and draw a tapered line following the tapered lines on the rear vertical measuring plane until it intersects the vertical lines of the left column and the vertical lines of the right column at H and I. Connect H with the near vanishing point VP and intersect the other vertical line at K. Thus we have constructed the columns on the first floor. We can also construct the counter, using the same method. First we draw its footprint on the floor measuring plane. Then we project all the vertical lines up, measure 1½ increments on the rear vertical measuring plane, which is 3'0" at L. Once we have located L, we can determine all the other points at the top of the counter.

We can construct the floor pattern on the floor measuring plane by simply counting the number of increments. The little complication here is the

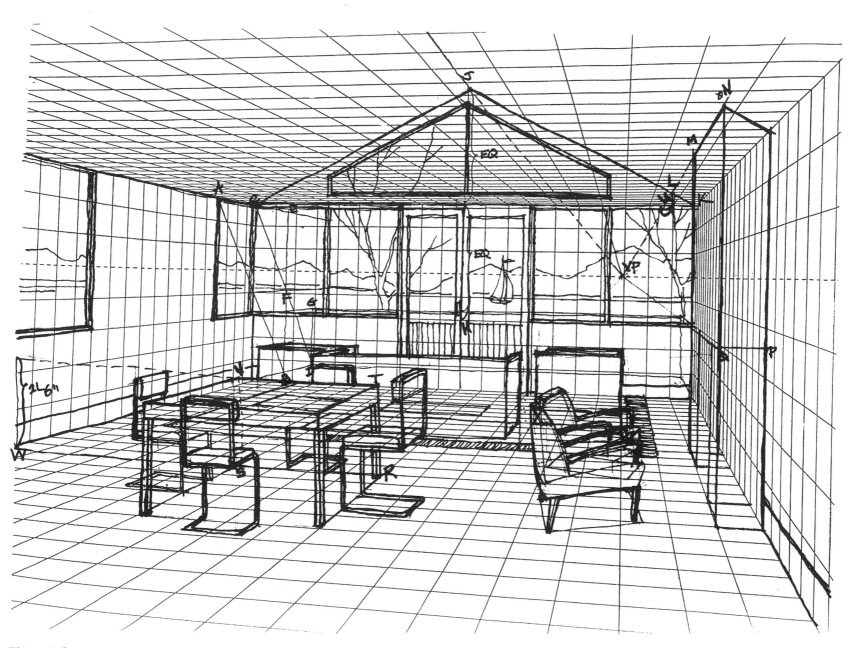

Figure 4-3

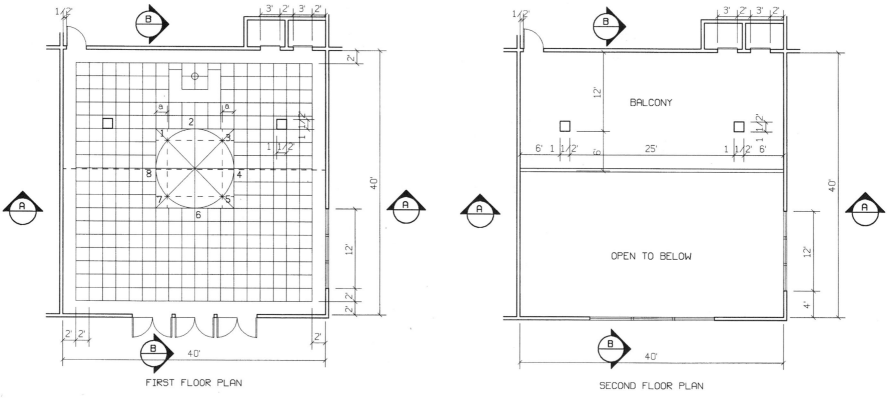

FIRST FLOOR PLAN

Figure 4-4

SECOND FLOOR PLAN

Figure 4-5

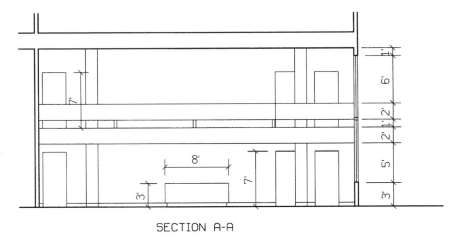

SECTION A-A

Figure 4-7

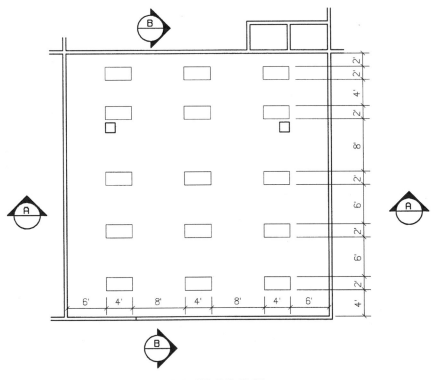

REFLECTED CEILING PLAN

Figure 4-6

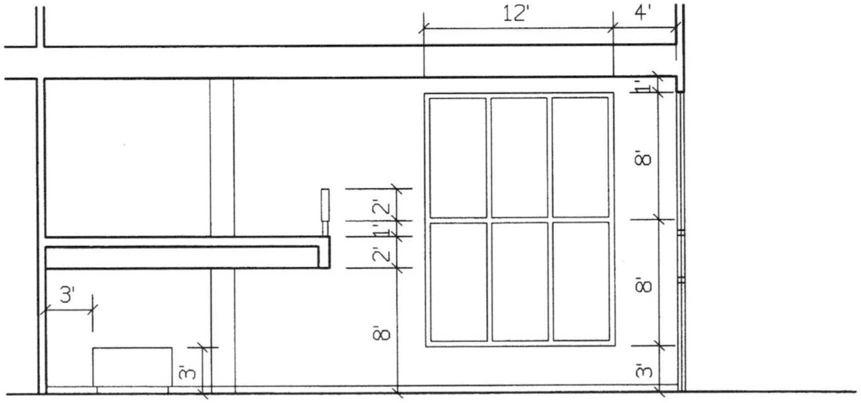

Figure 4-8

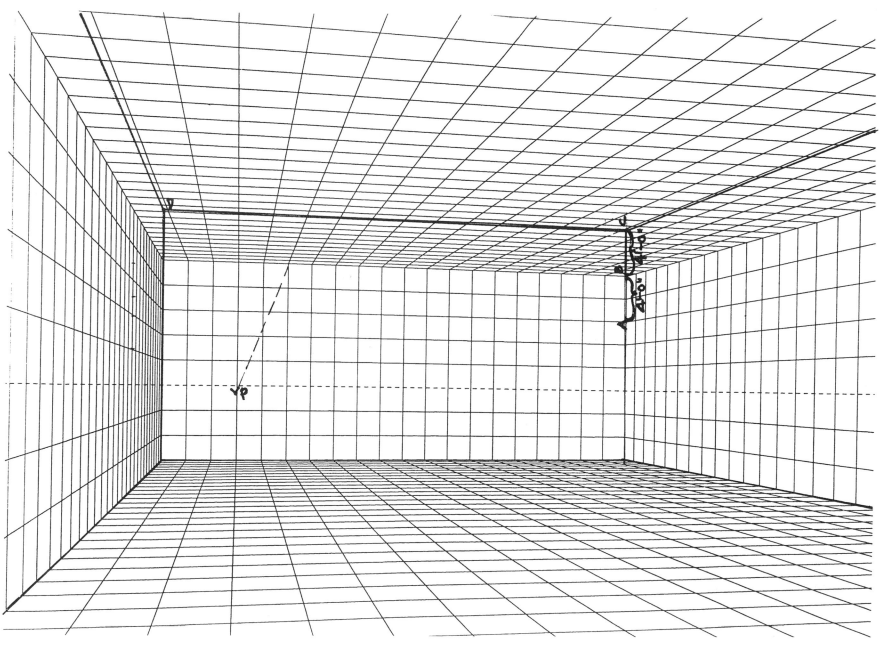

Figure 4-9

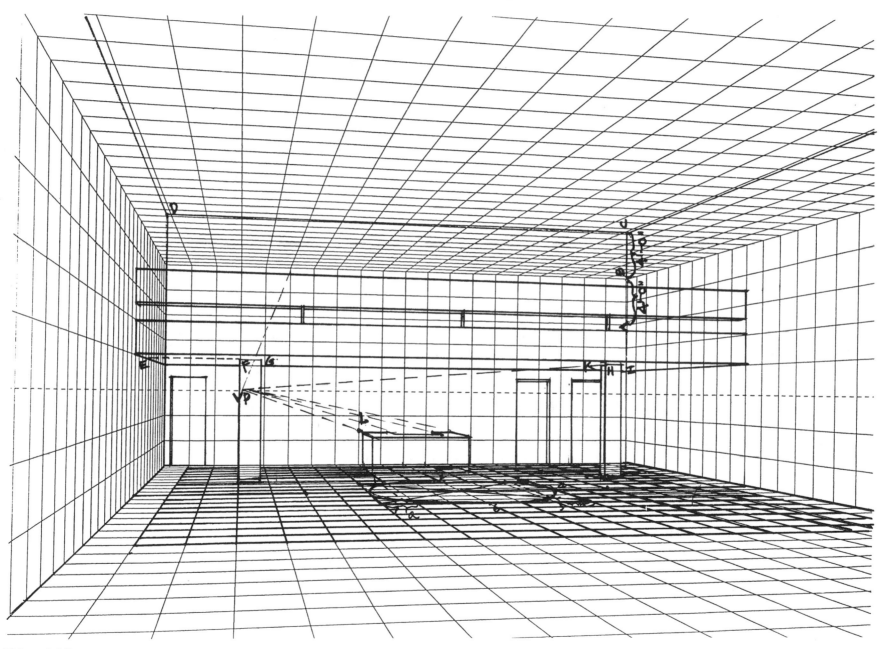

Figure 4-10

circular pattern on the center. Let's look at the floor plan (Fig. 4-4). To construct a circle, we always need to draw a square tangent to it. This square is already in our floor plan pattern. The two existing perpendicular diameters and two diagonal lines intersect the circle at points 1, 2, 3, 4, 5, 6, 7, and 8. We draw lines through 1 and 7 or 3 and 5, and we have a distance of a. Now we need to locate points 1, 2, 3, 4, 5, 6, 7, and 8 on the floor measuring plane. Points 2, 4, 6, and 8 are significant; they are the tangent points of the circle and the outer square. In the floor measuring plane, we measure distances of a from both ends of the tangent square, connect them to the near vanishing point VP, and intersect the two diagonal lines at 1, 3, 5, and 7. We now have eight points, which are enough to plot a circle. We use a French curve and connect the points and a circle in perspective is drawn.

In Fig. 4-11 we start to construct the columns on the second floor. From E we measure 1′6″ to M; from E and M we draw vertical lines until they intersect the ceiling line at M and O. We draw tapered lines following the tapered lines on the top measuring plane until they hit the extended vertical lines of the columns, and we have constructed the columns on the second floor.

To draw the elevator doors and the exit door on the second floor, we need to make some new measurements on the back wall. Let's divide BC into four 1′0″ marks. The doors are 3′0″ away from the ceiling line; therefore we count three 1′0″ marks down the ceiling and draw a tapered line until it intersects the vertical lines, and we have constructed the elevator doors. We can construct the exit door in the same manner.

The big windows on the left wall can be drawn by counting the increments on the left wall. For instance, it is 24′0″ from the back wall, so we just count 12 increments and we get to one side of the window. To construct the top of the window, we find the 1′0″ mark (one-half increment) down the ceiling on BC, draw a tapered line to VP, and extend it until it intersects the vertical lines of this window.

To construct the light fixtures on the ceiling, first extend 6′0″, 4′0″, 8′0″, 4′0″, 8′0″, and 4′0″ marks on the back wall until they touch the ceiling edge at P, Q, R, S, T, and U. Connect these points to VP and extend them along the ceiling, and we have the lengths of the light fixtures. We can locate the depths of the light fixtures in the same manner. Suppose that we want to locate the fourth row of light fixtures from the back wall. This row of lights is 6′0″ in front of the fascia of the balcony. Just count 3 increments, and draw a vertical line until it crosses V. The depths of the lights are 2′0″. Count another increment, and draw another vertical line until it crosses W. Draw tapered lines from V and W, until they hit the other tapered lines vanishing to VP, and we have constructed this row of light fixtures.

After the perspective is constructed, we can crop it in any way we want, as shown in Fig. 4-11.

A greater number of grids are included in this chapter to provide the user with the flexibility required in creating interior perspectives. Grids with 8, 9, 10, and 12 module heights are included, but you may want to turn the grids upside down to obtain additional horizon line options. For example, a grid with an 8 module height upside down can be used for a seated perspective.

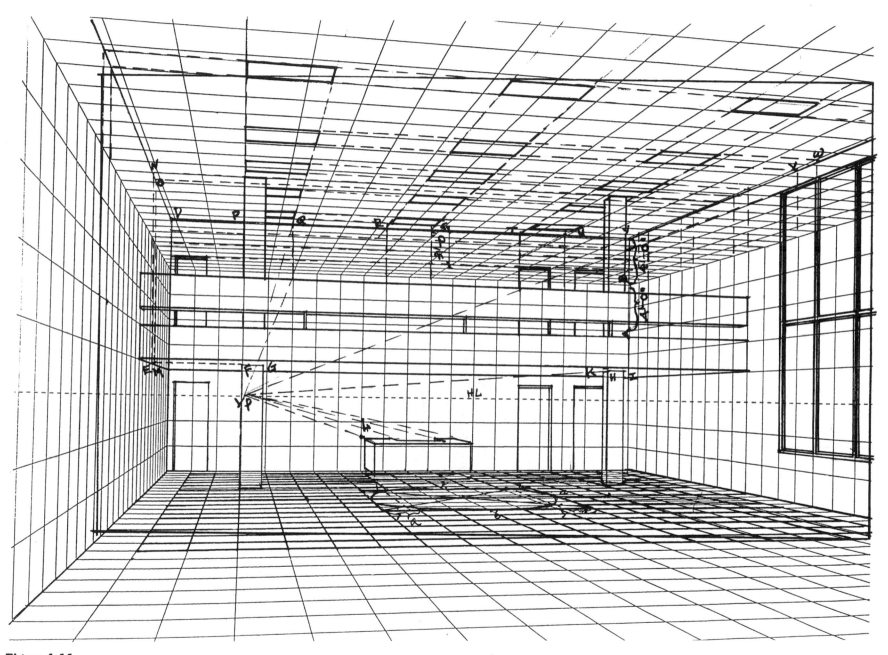

Figure 4-11

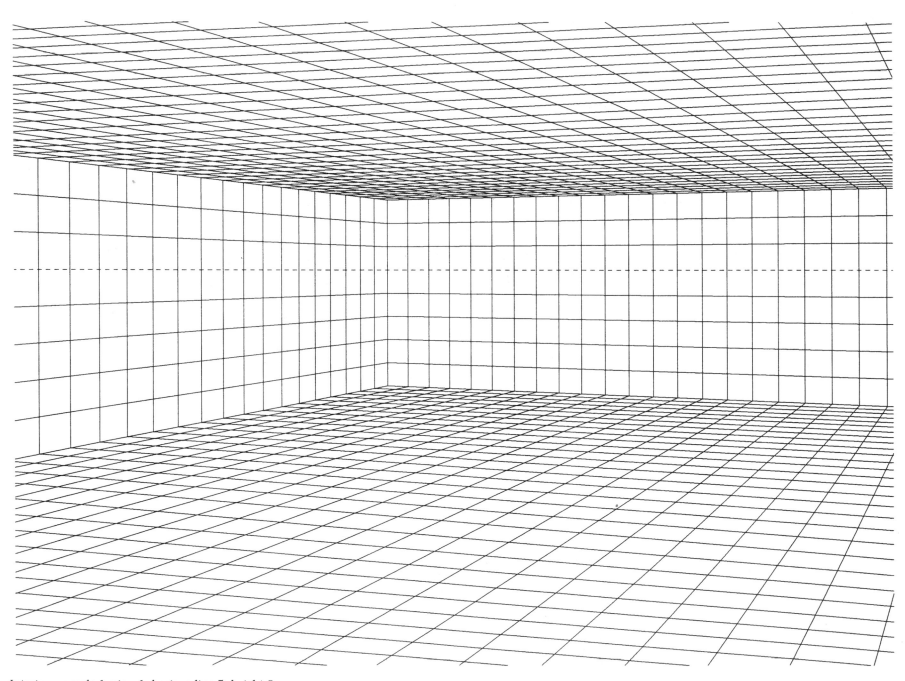

Interior example 1, view 1, horizon line 5, height 8.

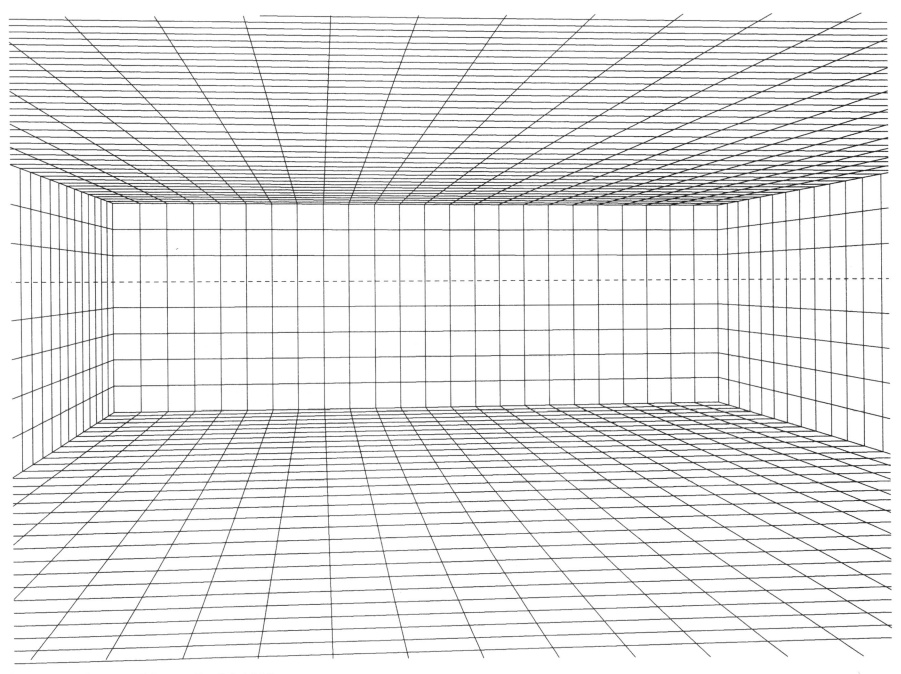

Interior example 1, view 5, horizon line 5, height 8.

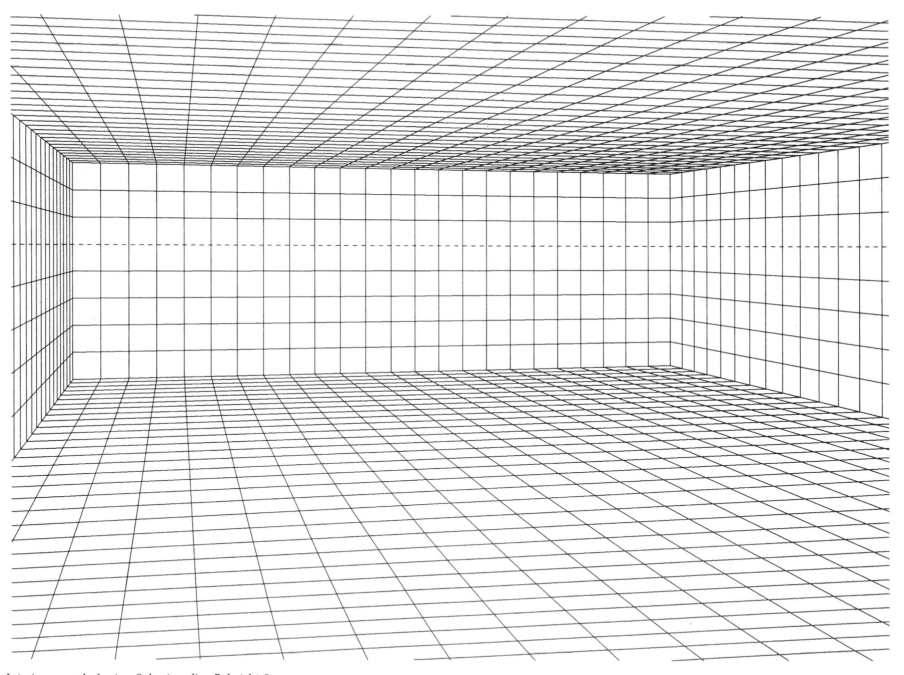

Interior example 1, view 6, horizon line 5, height 8.

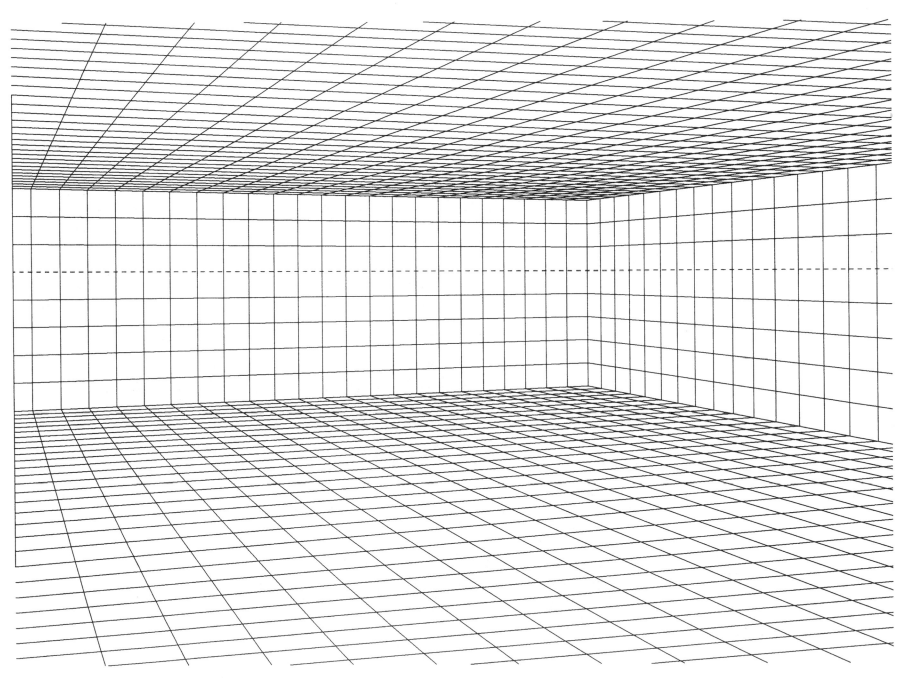

Interior example 1, view 7, horizon line 5, height 8.

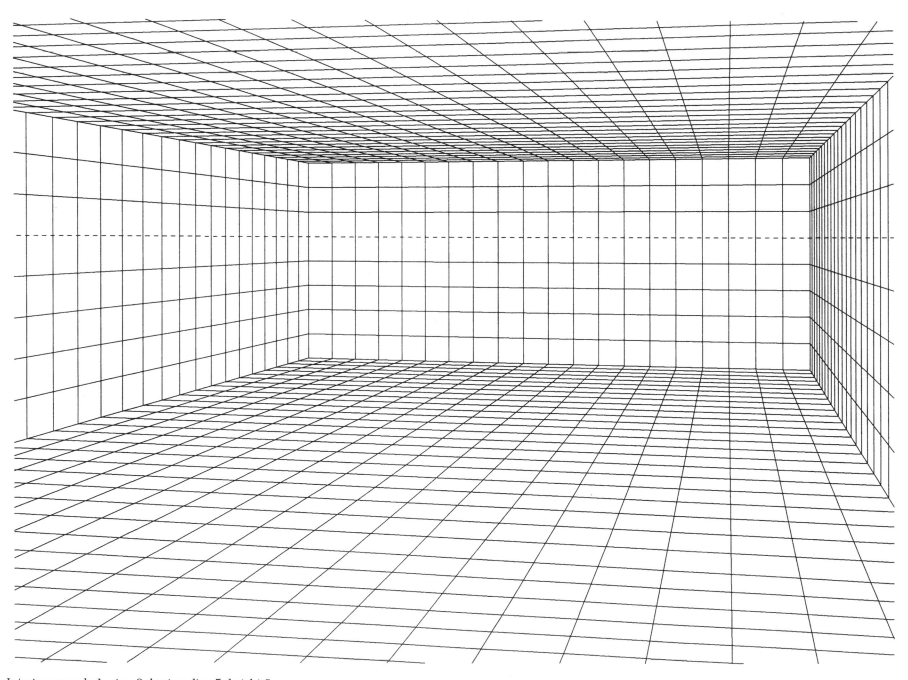

Interior example 1, view 8, horizon line 5, height 8.

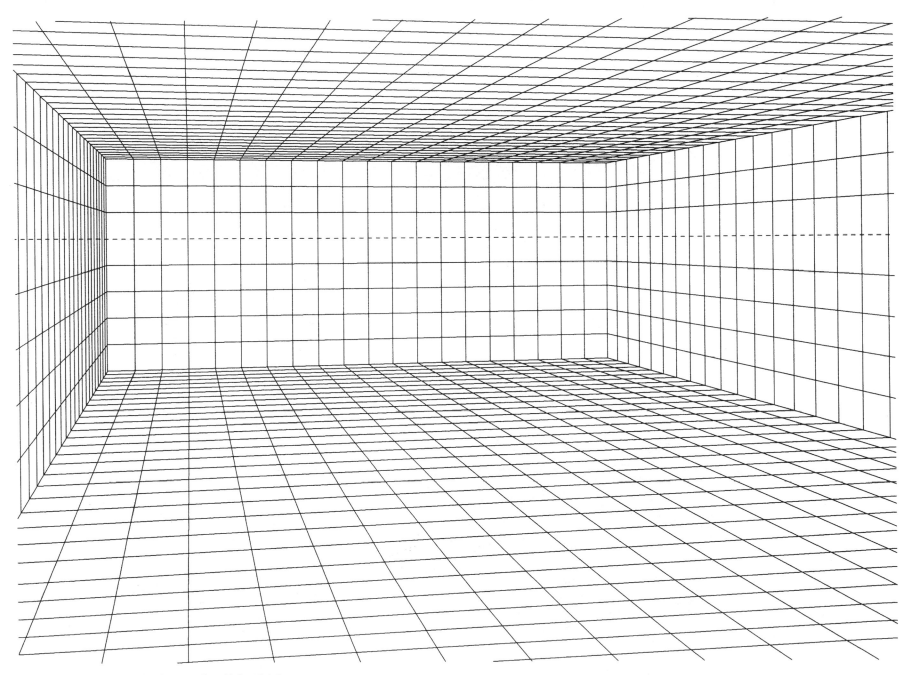

Interior example 1, view 10, horizon line 5, height 8.

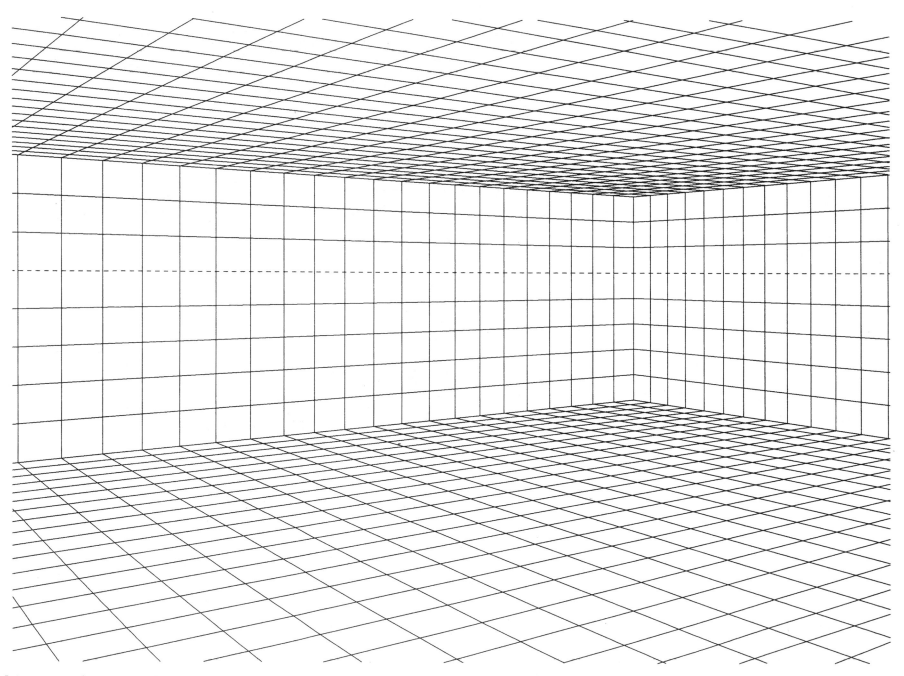

Interior example 1, view 14, horizon line 5, height 8.

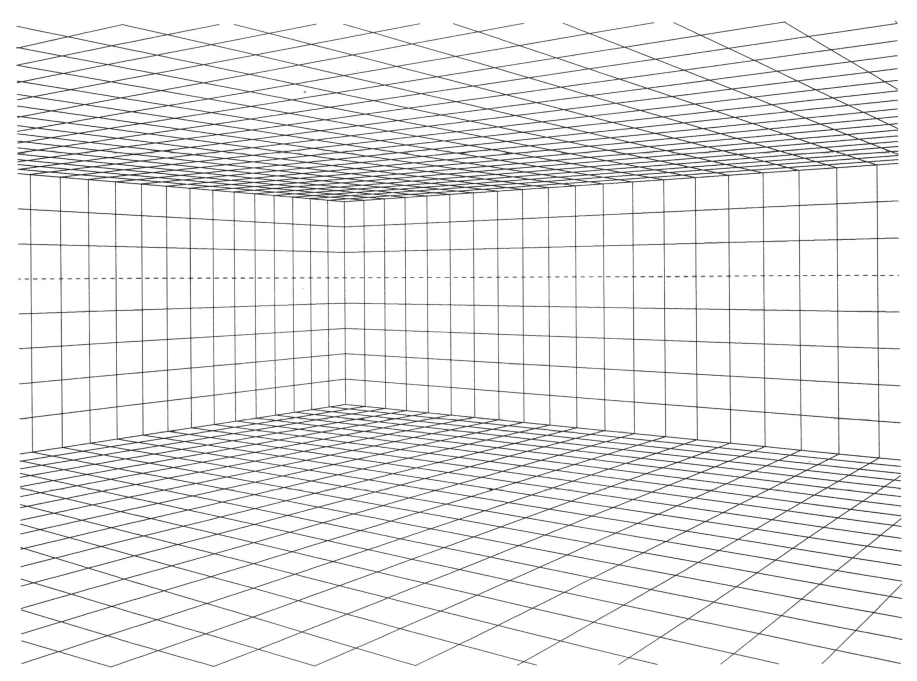

Interior example 1, view 15, horizon line 5, height 8.

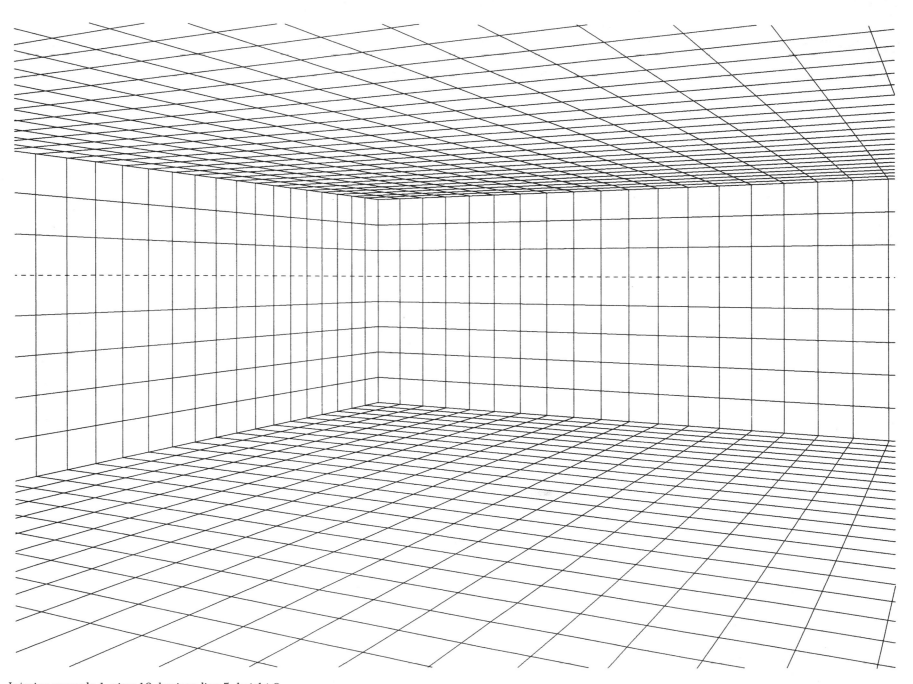

Interior example 1, view 16, horizon line 5, height 8.

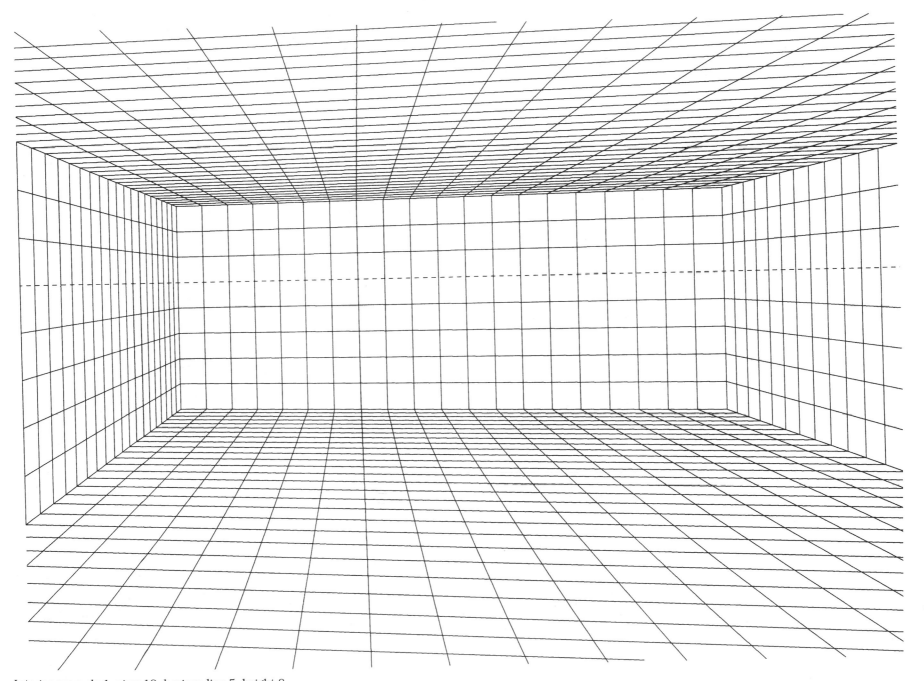

Interior example 1, view 18, horizon line 5, height 8.

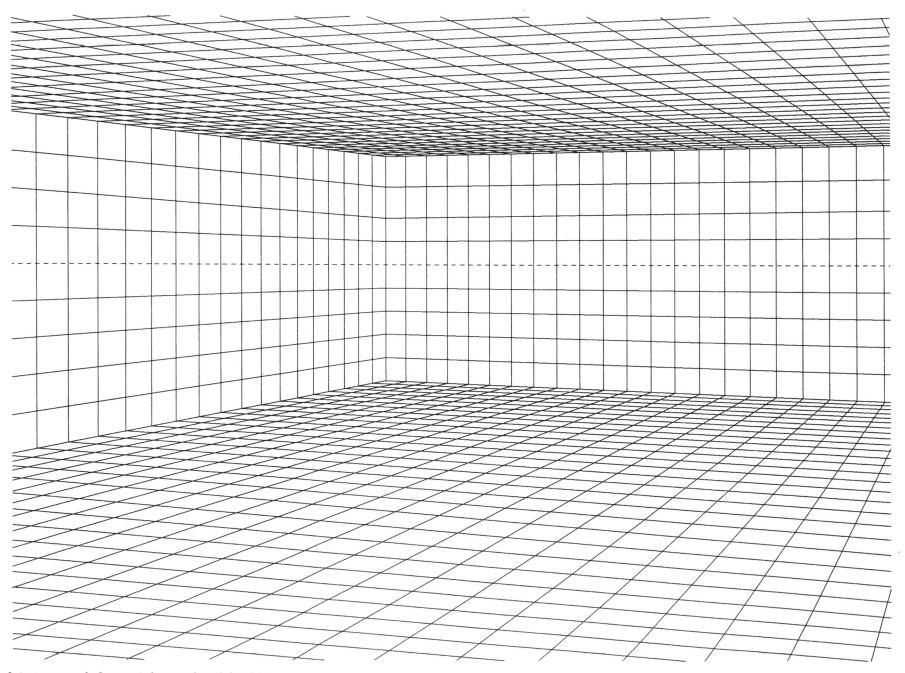

Interior example 2, view 1, horizon line 5, height 9.

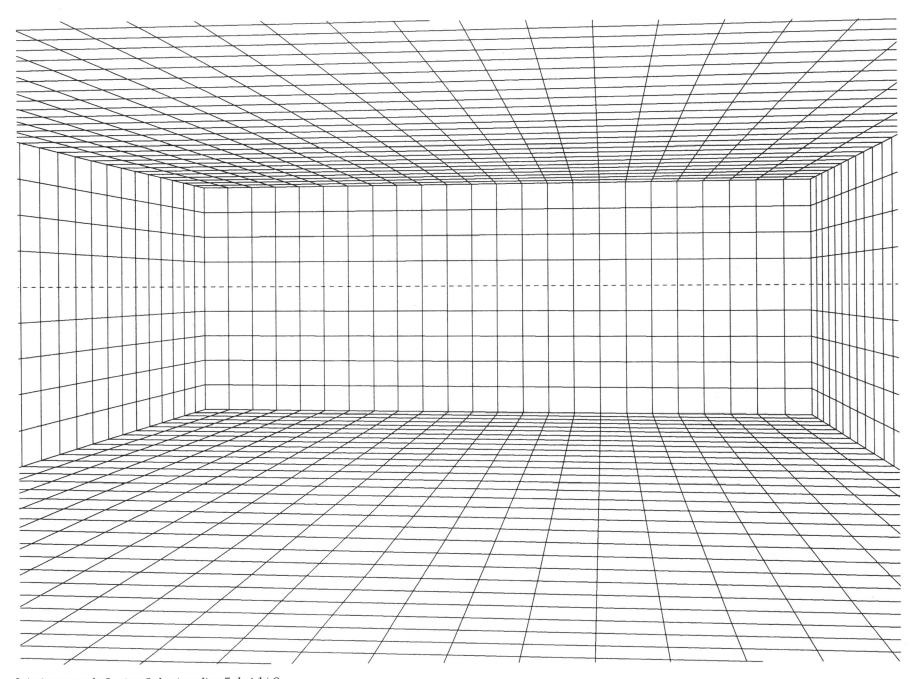

Interior example 2, view 3, horizon line 5, height 9.

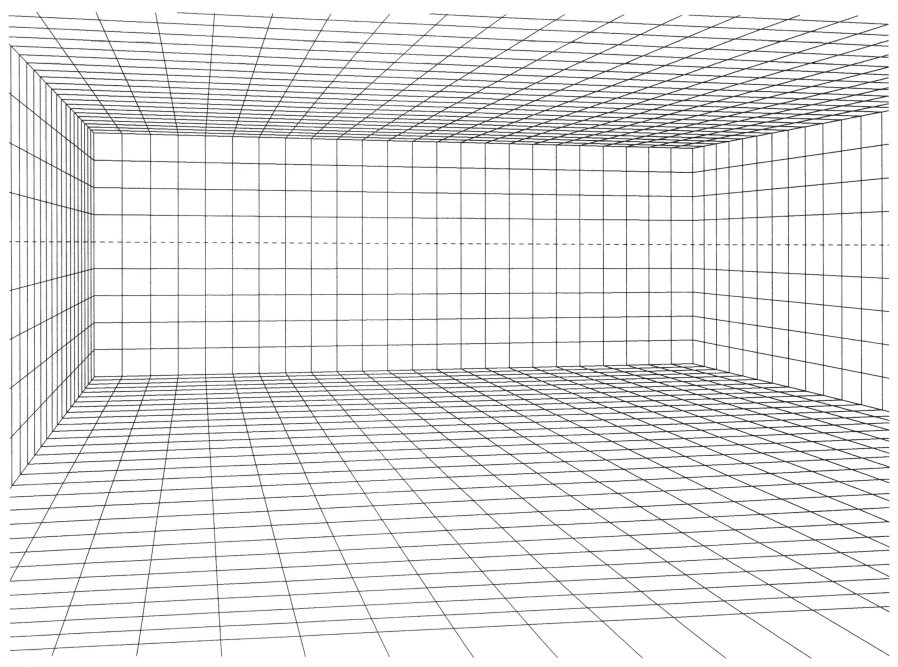

Interior example 2, view 6, horizon line 5, height 9.

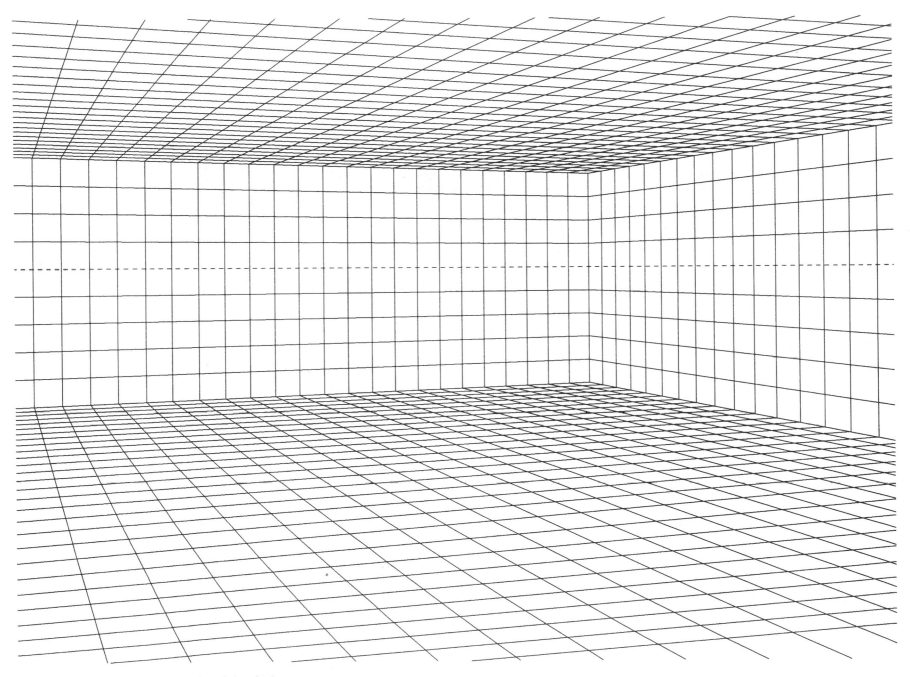

Interior example 2, view 7, horizon line 5, height 9.

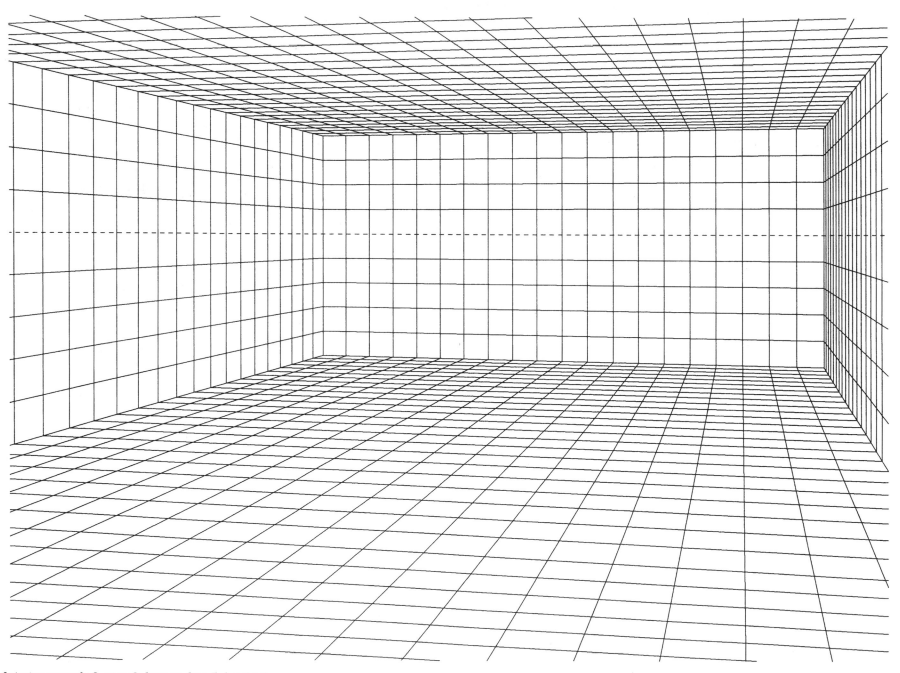

Interior example 2, view 8, horizon line 5, height 9.

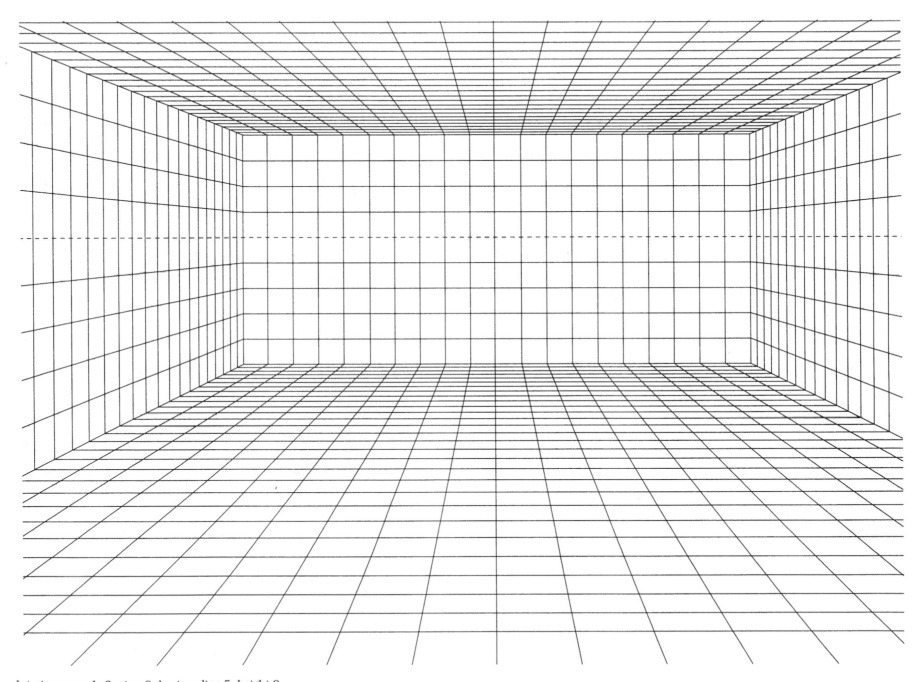

Interior example 2, view 9, horizon line 5, height 9.

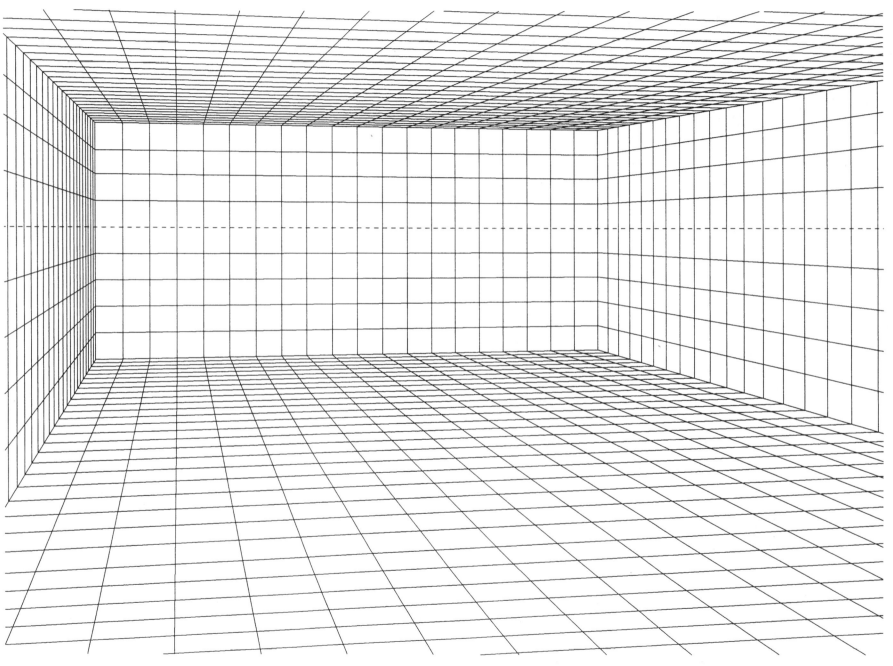

Interior example 2, view 10, horizon line 5, height 9.

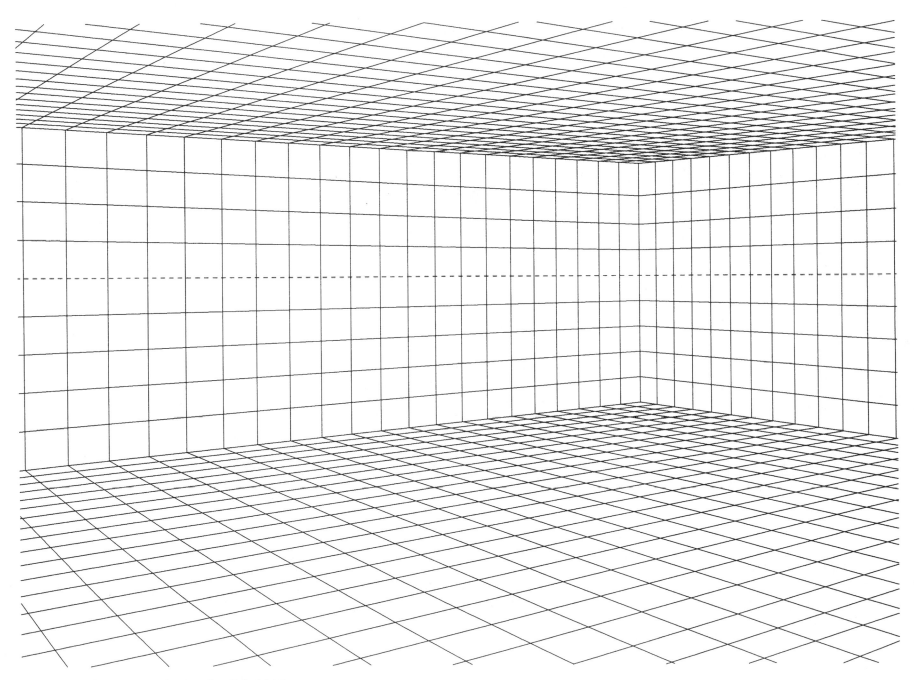

Interior example 2, view 14, horizon line 5, height 9.

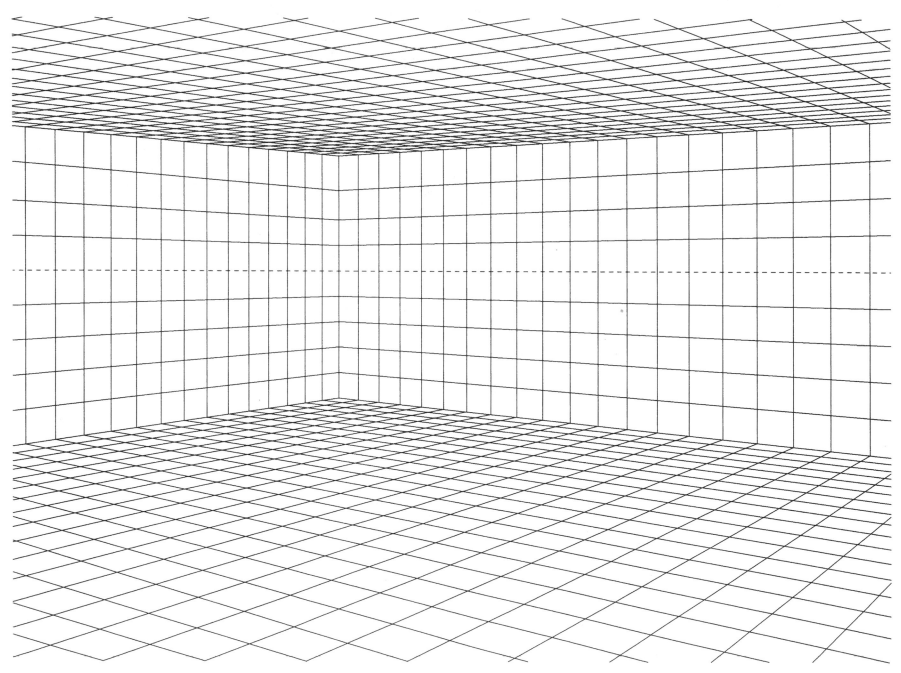

Interior example 2, view 15, horizon line 5, height 9.

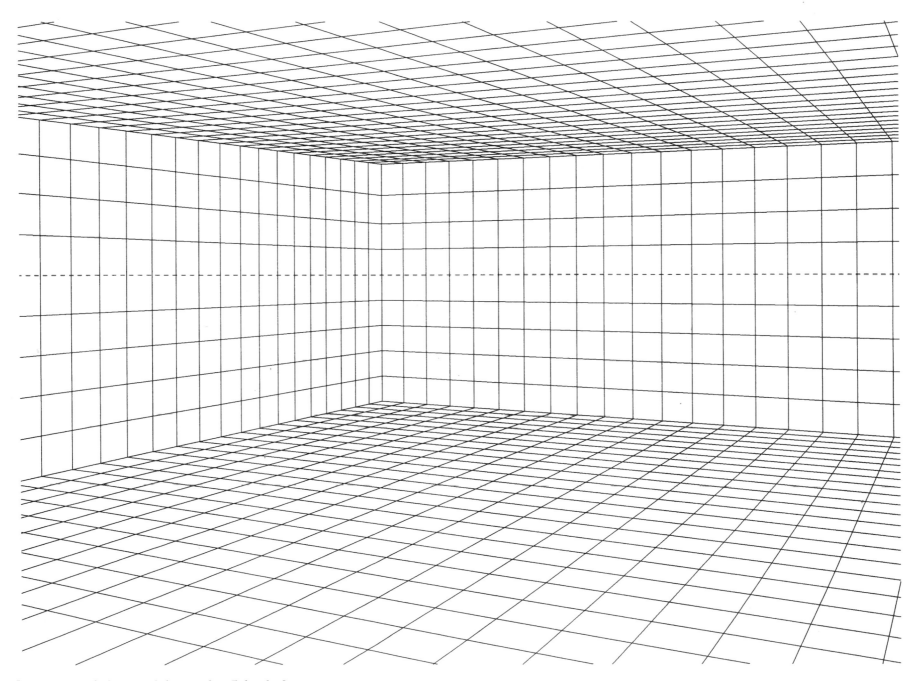

Interior example 2, view 16, horizon line 5, height 9.

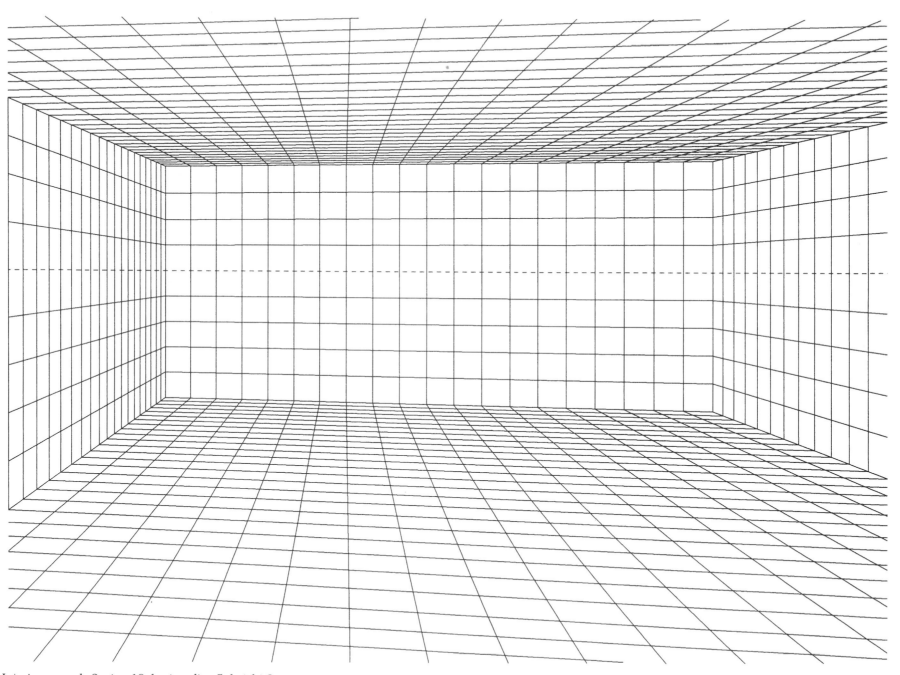

Interior example 2, view 18, horizon line 5, height 9.

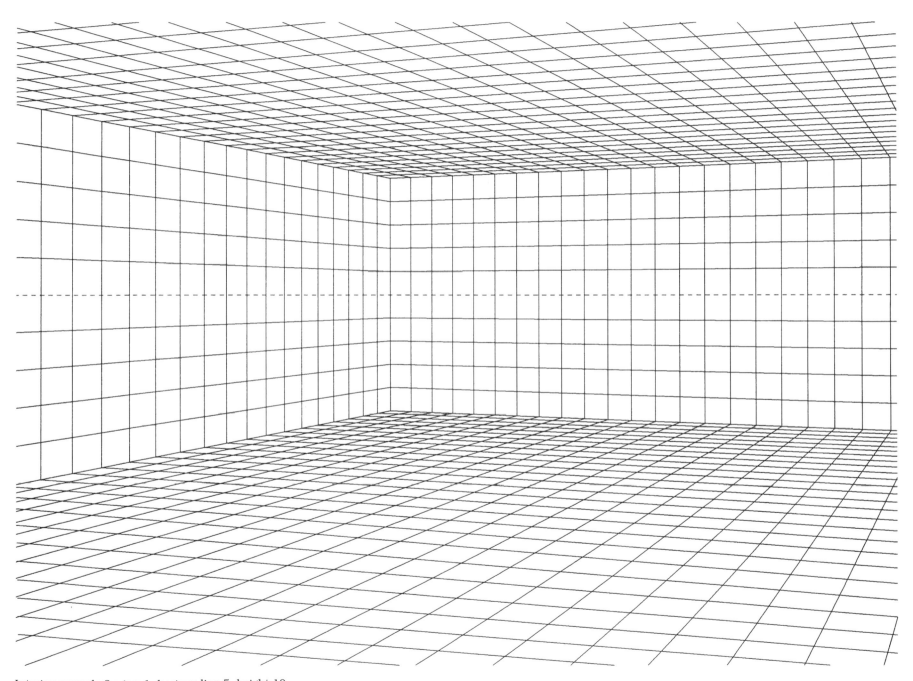

Interior example 3, view 1, horizon line 5, height 10.

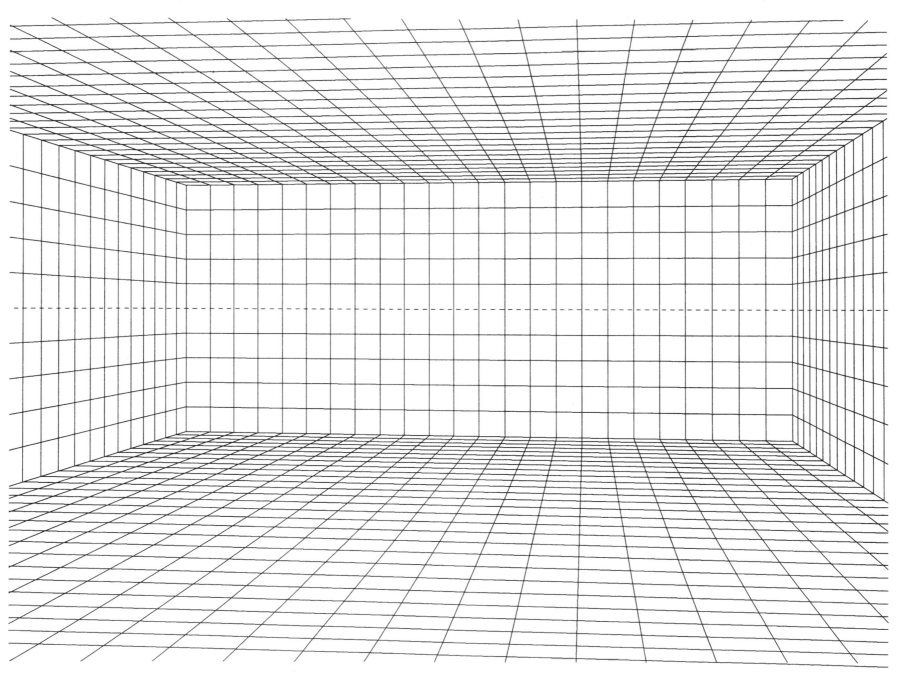

Interior example 3, view 3, horizon line 5, height 10.

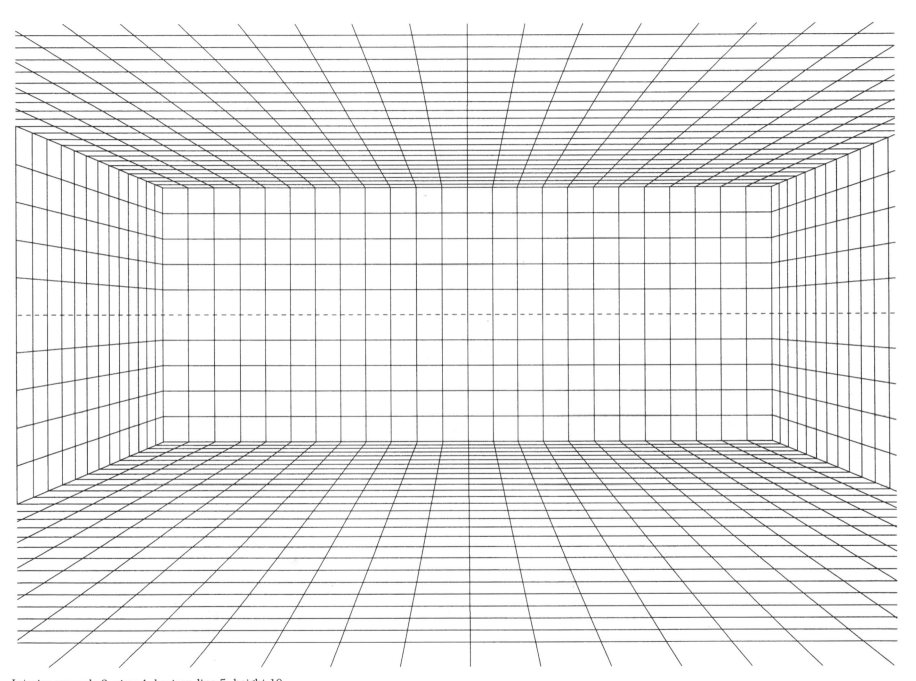

Interior example 3, view 4, horizon line 5, height 10.

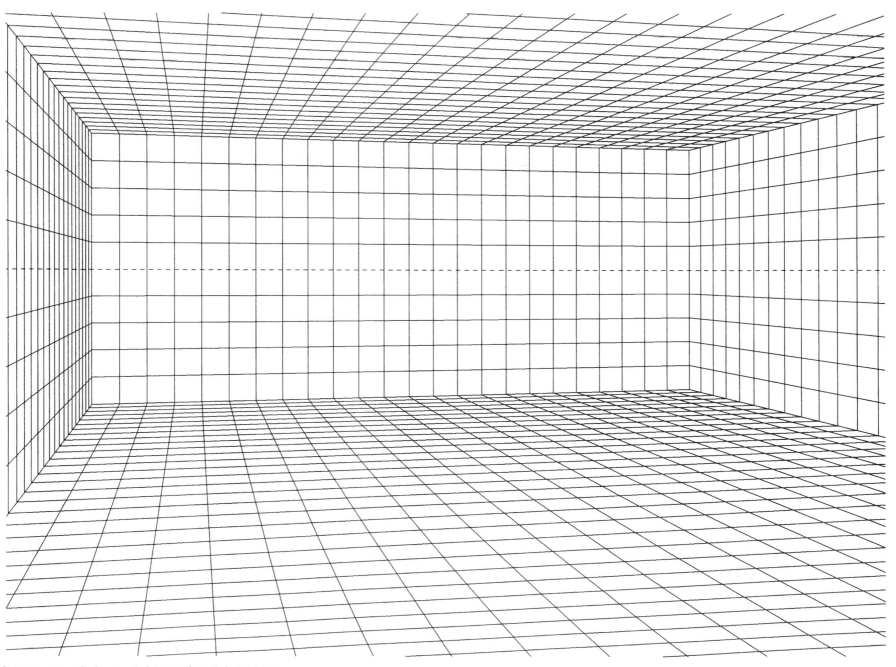

Interior example 3, view 6, horizon line 5, height 10.

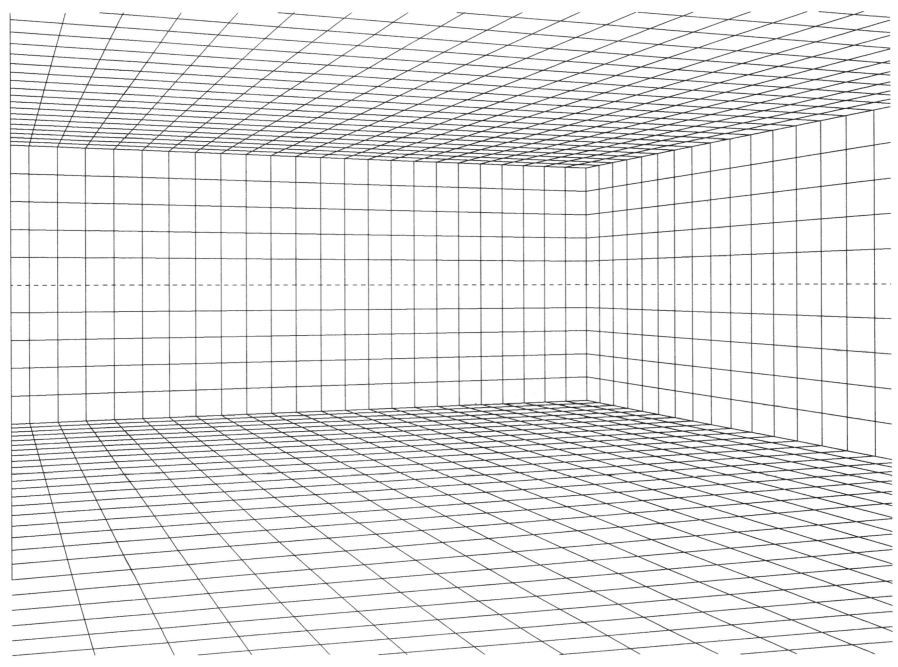

Interior example 3, view 7, horizon line 5, height 10.

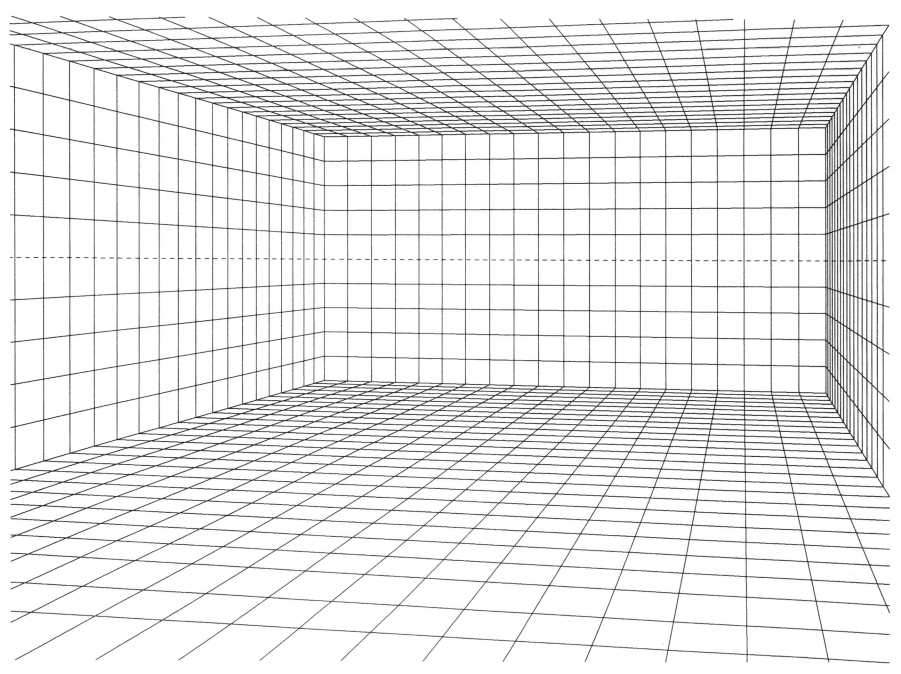

Interior example 3, view 8, horizon line 5, height 10.

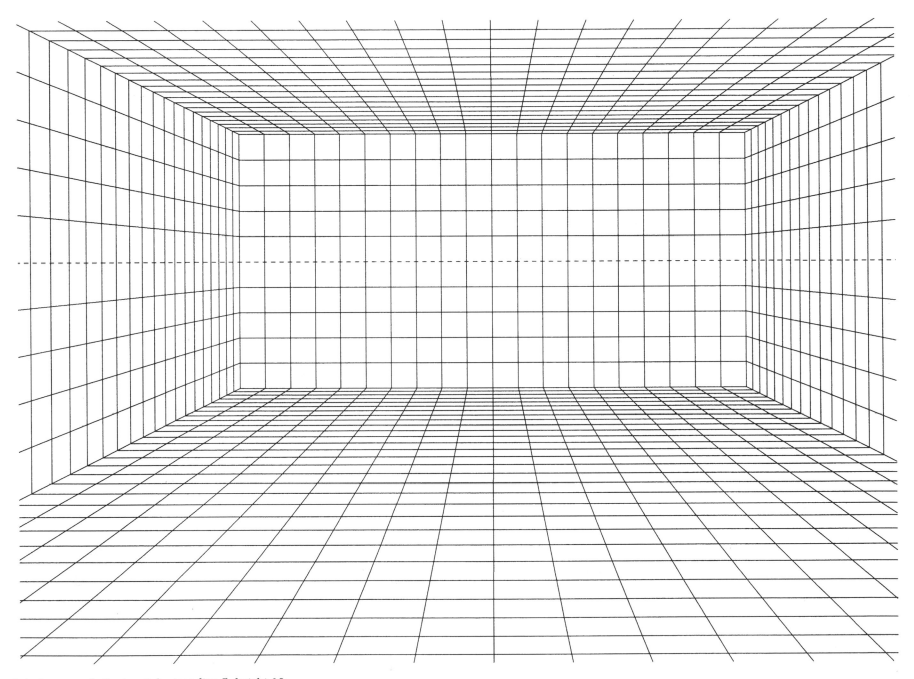

Interior example 3, view 9, horizon line 5, height 10.

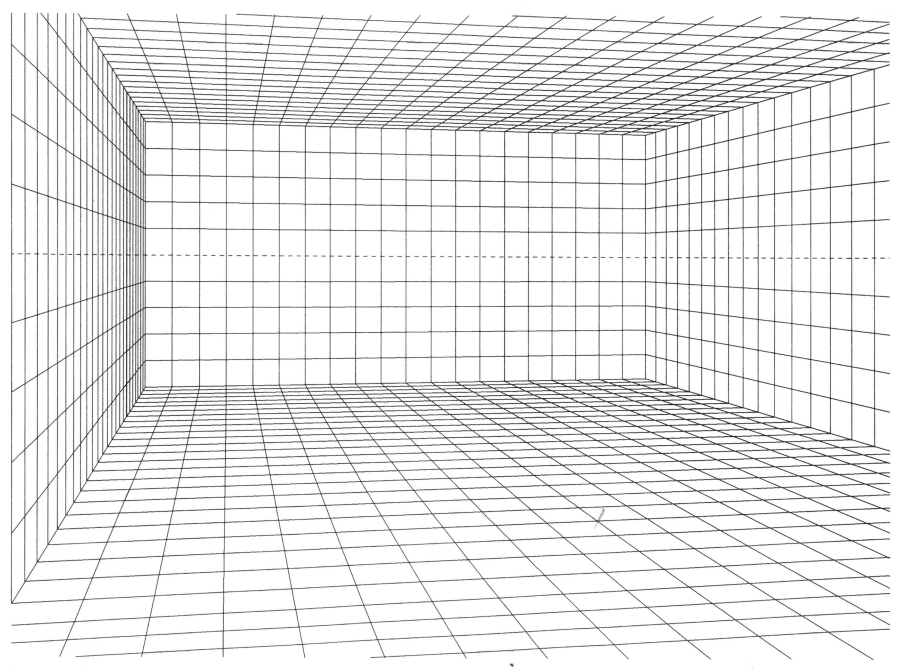

Interior example 3, view 10, horizon line 5, height 10.

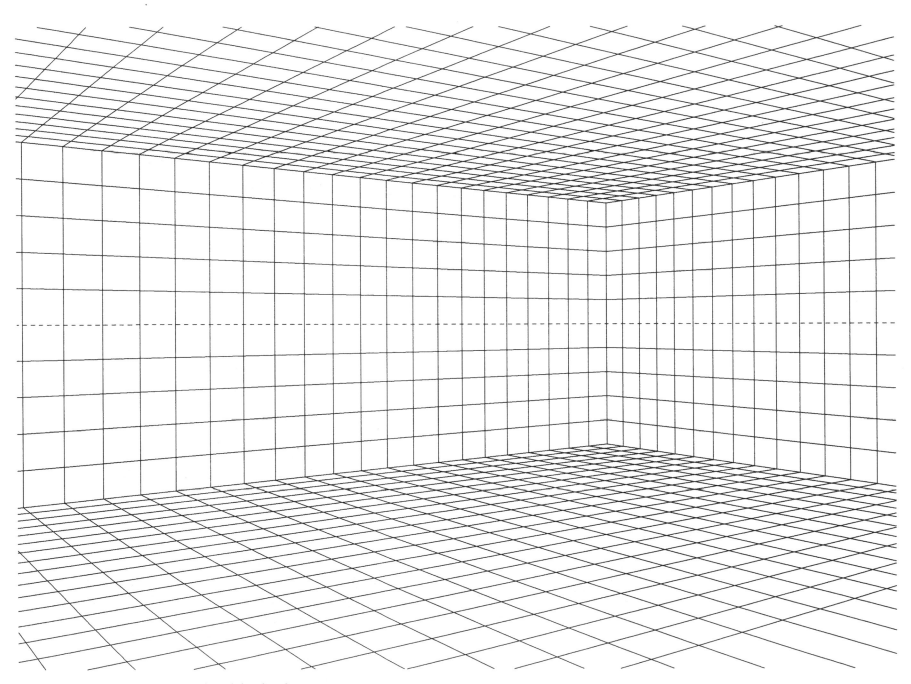

Interior example 3, view 14, horizon line 5, height 10.

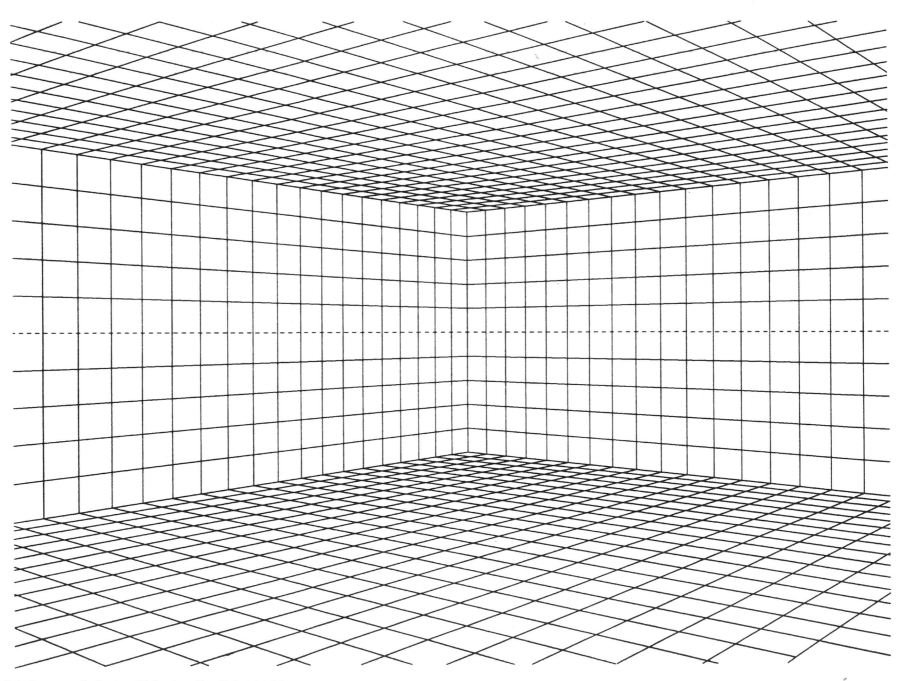

Interior example 3, view 15, horizon line 5, height 10.

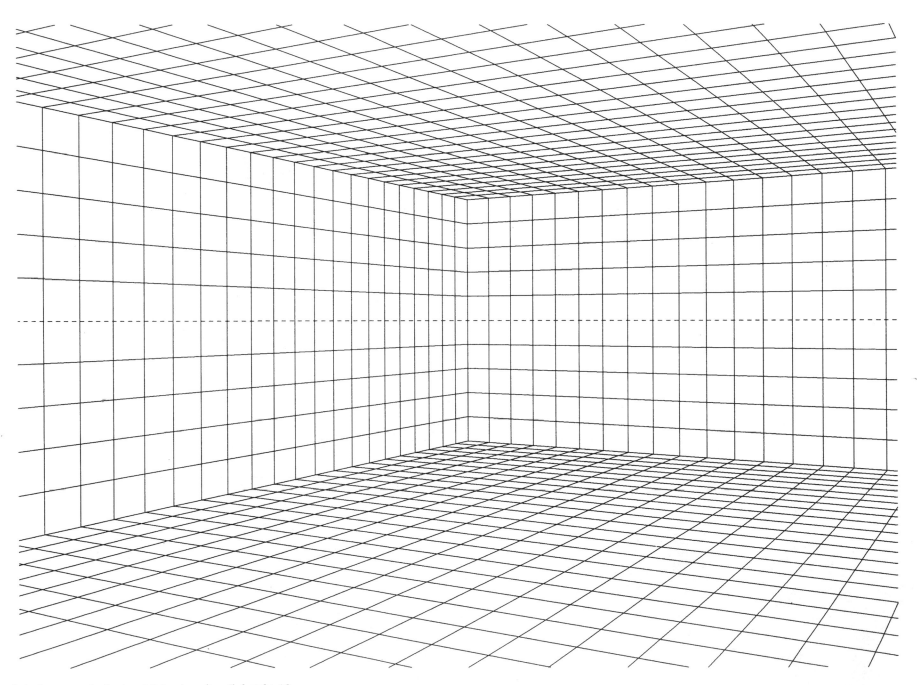

Interior example 3, view 16, horizon line 5, height 10.

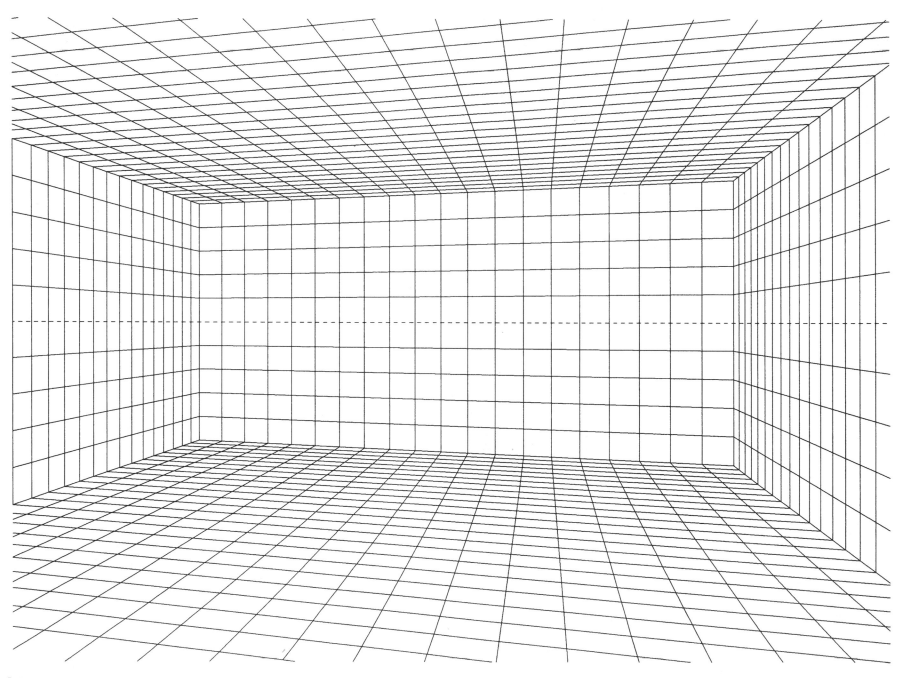

Interior example 3, view 17, horizon line 5, height 10.

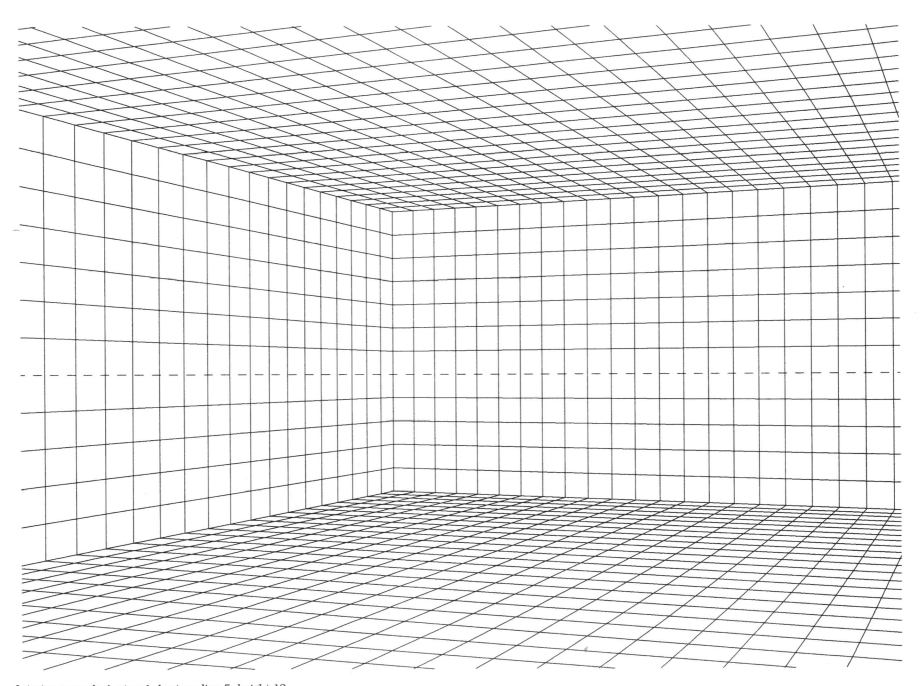

Interior example 4, view 1, horizon line 5, height 12.

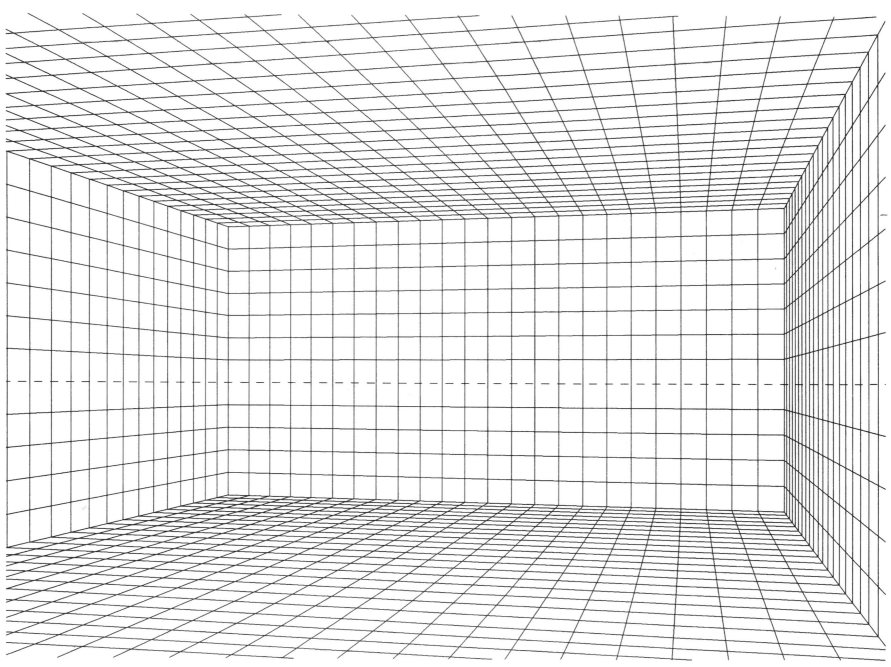

Interior example 4, view 2, horizon line 5, height 12.

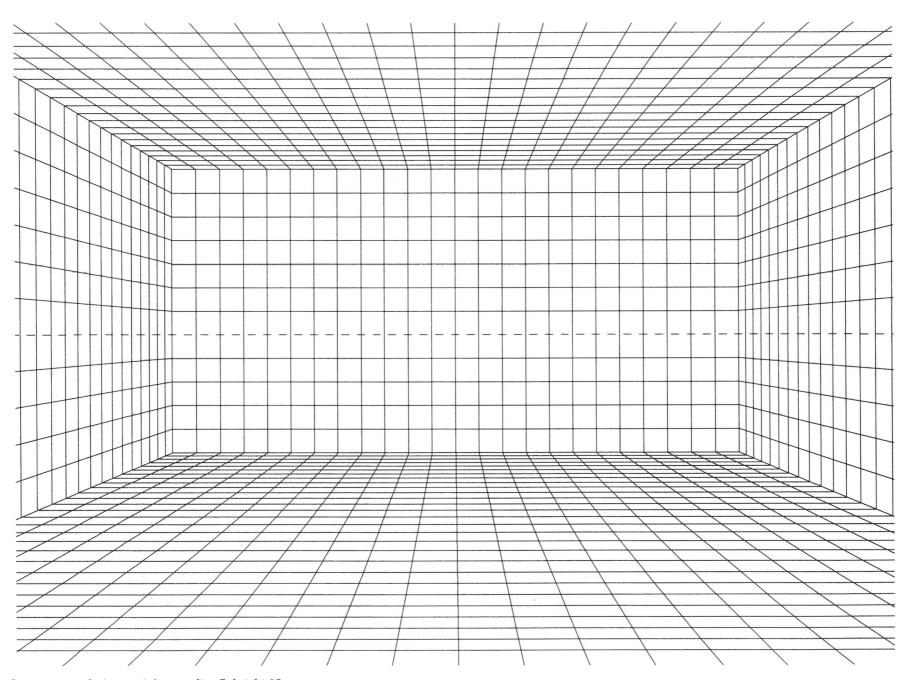

Interior example 4, view 4, horizon line 5, height 12.

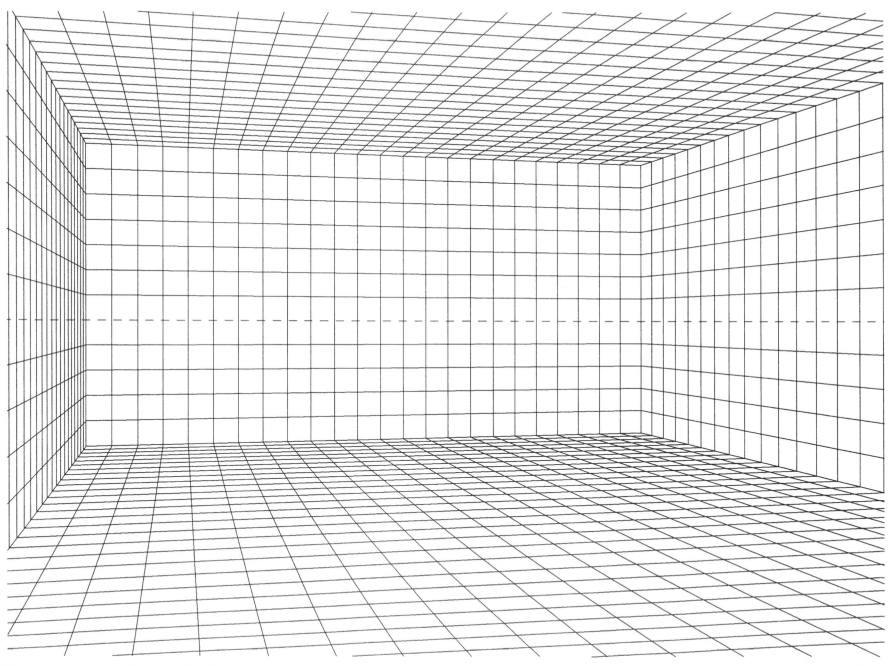

Interior example 4, view 6, horizon line 5, height 12.

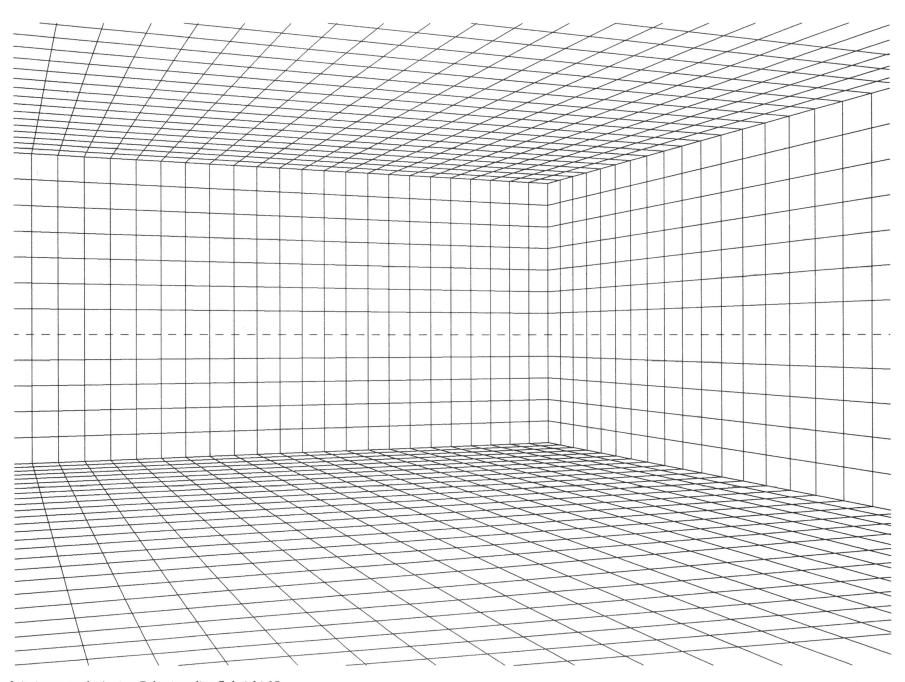

Interior example 4, view 7, horizon line 5, height 12.

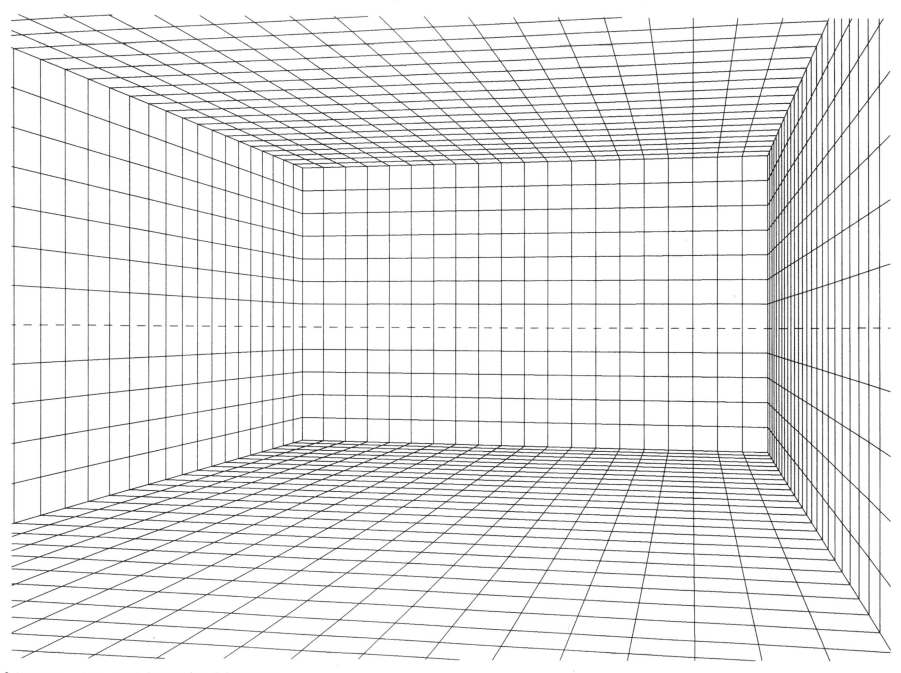

Interior example 4, view 8, horizon line 5, height 12.

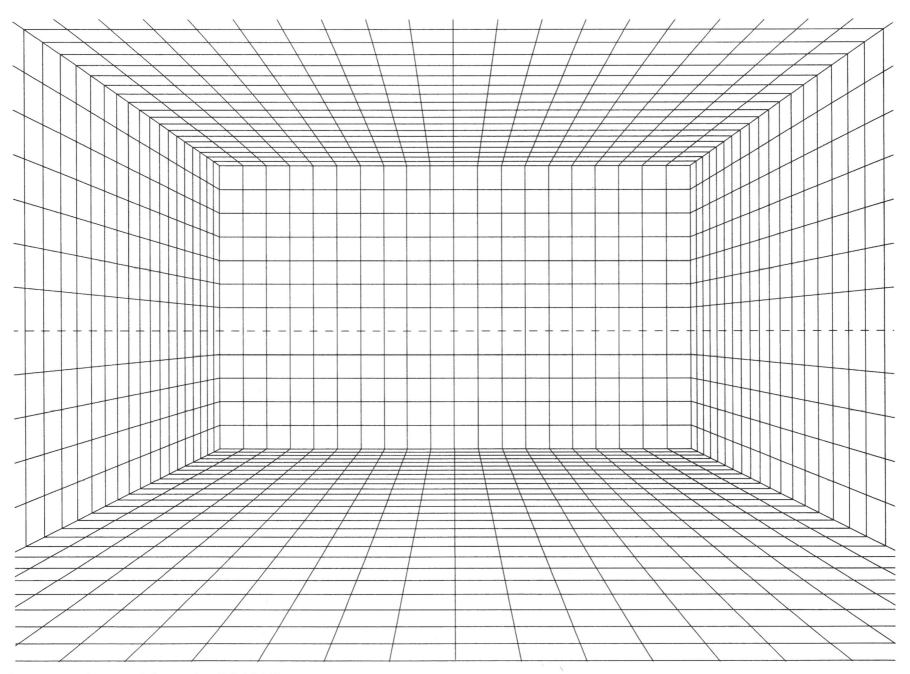

Interior example 4, view 9, horizon line 5, height 12.

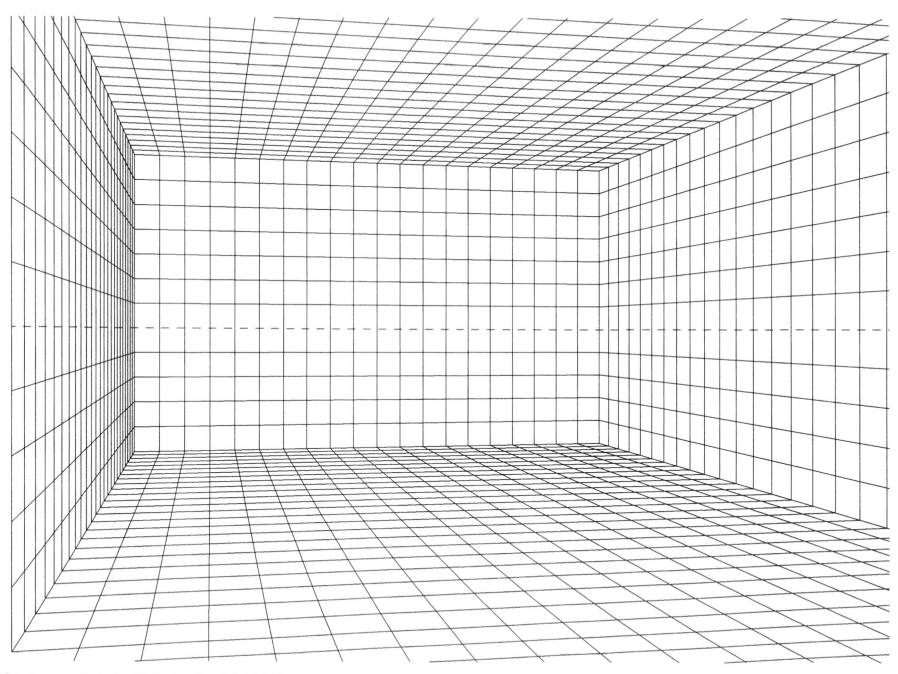

Interior example 4, view 10, horizon line 5, height 12.

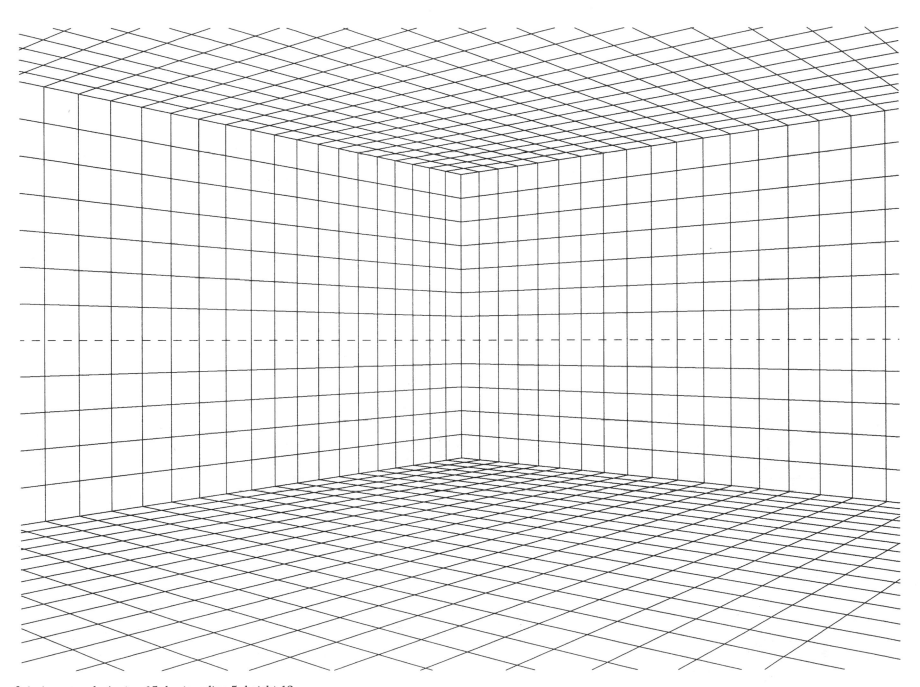

Interior example 4, view 15, horizon line 5, height 12.

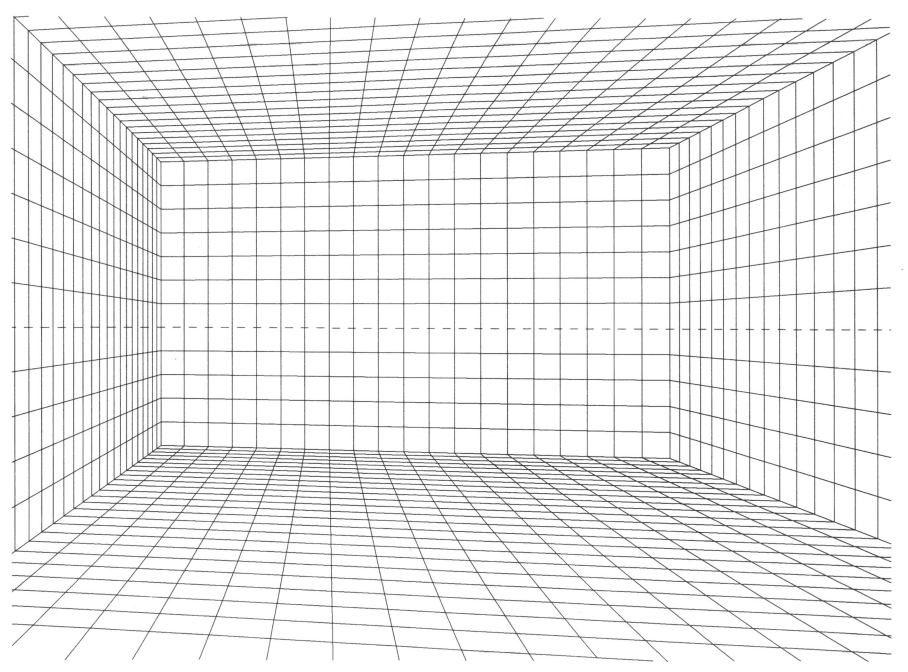

Interior example 4, view 18, horizon line 5, height 9.

Perspective Grids for Taller Building Design and Presentation

Taller buildings normally are larger buildings, have more details, and therefore are more difficult to design and present. In this chapter we introduce two kinds of perspective grids for use in taller building design and presentation: the two-point perspective grids and the three-point perspective grids. The two-point perspective grid has two vanishing points; its two groups of horizontal parallel lines vanish into their own vanishing points on the horizon line, and the vertical parallel lines remain vertical and parallel to each other. In reality, this is rarely the case, but since most drawings are drawn like that, it became acceptable to our eyes. The three-point perspective grid has a third vanishing point besides the two vanishing points located on the horizon line. This third vanishing point is located at a distant height; all vertical parallel lines vanish into this third vanishing point. Therefore the vertical lines in a three-point perspective are no longer parallel but taper toward each other. This is the actual situation when we look up at higher buildings from a lower altitude, such as when we stroll along the streets of Manhattan.

In an architectural perspective grid, the horizon line is shown as a dotted line. The vanishing points which are located on the horizon line are normally not shown in the grid drawing; they will land outside the drawing, especially in the taller building situation. Here we are using the result of a computer-drawn grid as a guideline. So we really do not need to know the locations of the vanishing points or of the station point; because as long as the angle of the grid looks acceptable, we can just use it for our design or presentation.

Figures 5-1 to 5-7 show the consecutive steps of a three-dimensional design of a condominium complex in San Francisco. The project is composed of an 80'0" by 80'0" (planar measurement) luxurious condominium tower and a 110'0" by 120'0" (planar measurement) base with health spas, celebrity shops, and restaurants. The project hopes to attract wealthy Asians to live in the heart of San Francisco. Due to this situation the units are larger than usual. The penthouse unit comprises the top two floors and costs a few million dollars.

Figure 5-1 shows the massing of the condominium complex. Here we assign 3'4" to each increment, so 3 increments equal 10'0". It is advisable that we mark every 10'0" on the grid if we can, for this will make it much easier and more accurate to design or plot the building on the grid. First we plot the footprints of the tower and the base on the floor measuring plane, and then we draw the volumes of the tower and its base. Let's assume that the floor-to-floor height of the tower is 10'0". Then we can indicate all the 10'0" lines on the grid. Let's say that the base consists of two floors, each 15'0" high. The height of the base is 30'0" plus a parapet height of 3'4" which totals to 33'4". To meet certain requirements, the building is not to exceed a height of 236'8", which includes two base floors, 20 condominium floors, and a top parapet of 6'8". By matching the dimension marks on the grid we can easily draw the overall volume of the building.

After the volume of the building is drawn, we notice that it has exceeded the floor-area ratio (FAR) requirement. And because this is a corner building and there are other concerns for planning regulations, we have

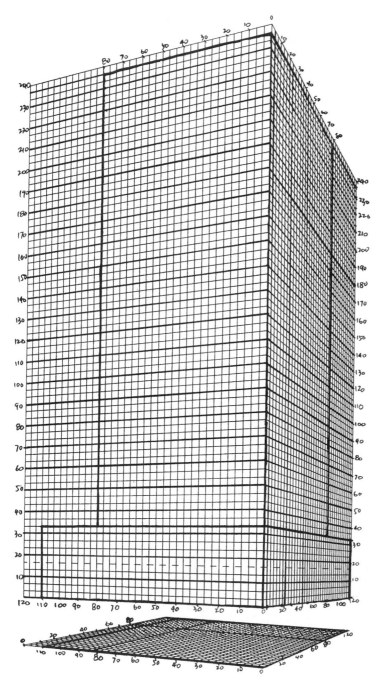

Figure 5-1

decided to do some "sculpturing" work, mainly at the right corner of the building. A step-back feature is chosen which will make the square footage of the building match the required FAR. Actually, we can design as many schemes for this project as possible, but to save space we have decided to show just three schemes. Before we put the final details into the design, we should draw the general configuration of the building. Figure 5-2 is a straight-corner scheme, Fig. 5-3 is a rounded-corner scheme, and because this project is located in San Francisco, a bay window scheme (Fig. 5-4) is also considered.

To work out the configuration of the building, we integrate the design of the floor plan closely with the design of the elevations. For instance, when we design the straight-corner scheme in Fig. 5-2, we first plot the side elevation on the right, because the step-back feature happens on the right measuring plane (measuring grid). It is harder to plot something that is not on the measuring plane. Let's say we want to plot point B. We can first draw a tapered line from S following the tapered lines that vanish to the far vanishing point. Then we project a perpendicular line from C on the floor measuring plane; the intersection of these two lines is point B. We can also do it another way by drawing a tapered line from A following the tapered lines that vanish to the near vanishing point, and the intersection of AB and BS is B. Notice here that A and S are at the same height of 193'4", which is the 18th floor plus a parapet height. If we want to plot point H on the upper left corner, we first draw a tapered line from G following the tapered lines on the right measuring plane that vanish to the near vanishing point, and we project a perpendicular line from point D. The intersection is point H.

Using the same method, we can also work out the configuration of the rounded-corner scheme in Fig. 5-3 and the bay window scheme in Fig. 5-4. In the rounded-corner scheme we can first treat it as a straight-corner scheme, and because of the scale of the drawing we just estimate its curvature.

After the basic configuration of the schemes has been designed, we can start to plot the details (Figs. 5-5, 5-6, and 5-7). Note here that all the window bands of the tower are 6'8" high, which equals 2 increments, and the wall bands are 3'4" high, which equals 1 increment. Since this is a condominium complex, a series of balconies can be cut into the building according to its function and aesthetics. For instance, Fig. 5-7 is a scheme which mixes bay windows with balconies. The scale of the details of any of these schemes can be easily determined by relating them to the dimension marks on the grid.

The two sides of the base of the building are both on the measuring plane; therefore they can be designed easily from the dimension marks

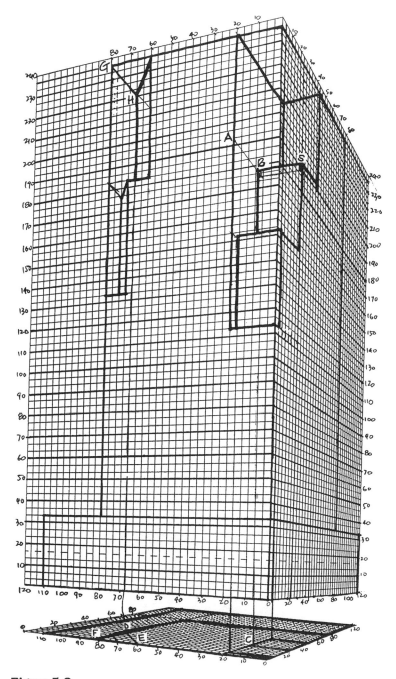

Figure 5-2

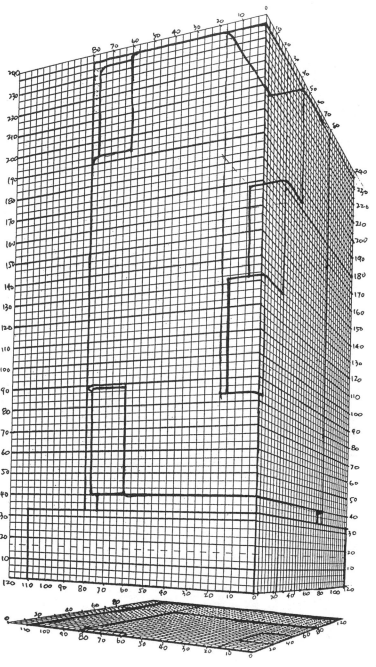

Figure 5-3

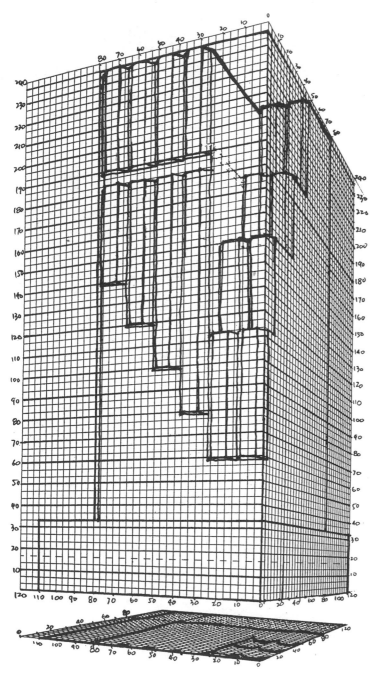

Figure 5-4

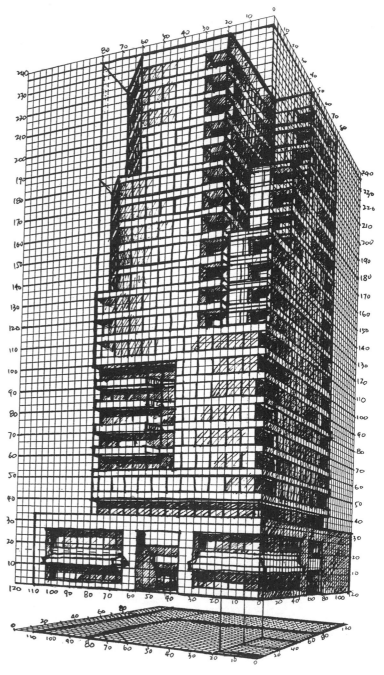

Figure 5-5

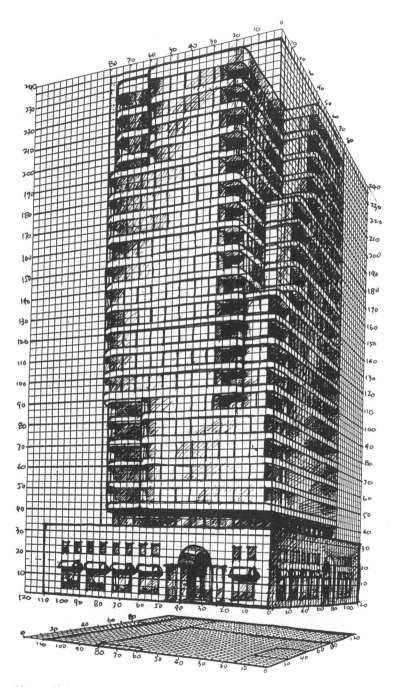

Figure 5-6

Figure 5-7

on the grid. After we have plotted the wire frame of the three schemes, we can add a little texture and shading if we feel it is needed. This will make the design look more three-dimensional.

The second example uses a three-point perspective grid to design a high-rise mixed-use commercial building with a 4-story shopping mall and a 60-story office tower. The process of the design is quite similar to that of the previous example. First we assign a scale to the grid. Let's say the floor-to-floor height of the office tower is 12'0", the floor-to-floor height of the shopping mall is 15'0", and the overall height of the building is somewhere around 820'0" (excluding the pinnacle). Here, the easiest approach is to make each increment 24'0", which represents 2 stories of office space or 1½ stories of shopping space. Once we decide on the scale of the increments, it is advisable to indicate the dimension marks on the grid wherever necessary.

The next step is to plot the estimated volume of the building (Fig. 5-8). The footprint of the building is 144'0" by 144'0". The 64-story building has a total height of 816'0". This volume can be easily plotted by following the dimension marks on the grid. The three-point perspective grid normally does not come with a floor measuring plane, so we must try to plot everything on the elevation measuring planes. For points not located on the elevation measuring planes, we have to use the intersection of the tapered line method. Suppose we want to find the back corner point D. We first draw a tapered line from A following the vanishing lines on the right measuring plane until it intersects the tapered line from C following the vanishing lines on the left measuring plane. This intersection point is point D. To find the center of the tower E (where the pinnacle is growing from), simply draw diagonal lines AC and BD; the intersection of these two diagonal lines occurs at E.

Figure 5-9 shows how we can match the FAR and make the building more interesting by trimming, twisting, and turning parts of the building. In this book we do not discuss the aesthetics of design. We just show how three-dimensional design can be achieved by using the computer-generated grids. There can be hundreds of different solutions to the same problem. In our example, let's plot the points on the elevation measuring planes, and the rest of the points can be plotted by using the example mentioned in Fig. 5-8. Thus we have completed the configuration of the building.

The next step is to draw some details into the building. Since this is a schematic design, it is not necessary for every line to be indicated (Fig. 5-10). Shading the building will make the building look more three-dimensional and more real (Fig. 5-11).

As in previous chapters, a representative group of grids follows. It is recommended that the reader explore the use of the additional grids provided on the book's accompanying disk.

Chapters 1 through 5 have shown us that computer-generated grids can be used for many purposes. Besides site design, exterior design, and interior design, they can be used for streetscape design and detail design. For instance, the interior perspective grids will also be applicable for streetscape design. Detail design can use either the interior or the exterior grids. If we flip the site grid upside down, we can use it for ceiling design or presentation. Other nonarchitectural designs also use these grids as a tool for three-dimensional design or presentation. It is up to the user to explore and create endless uses for these grids.

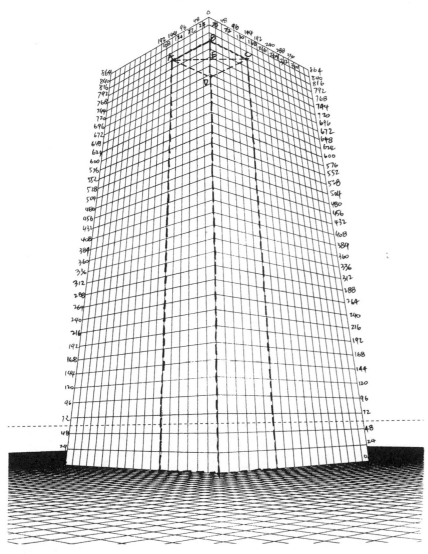

Figure 5-8

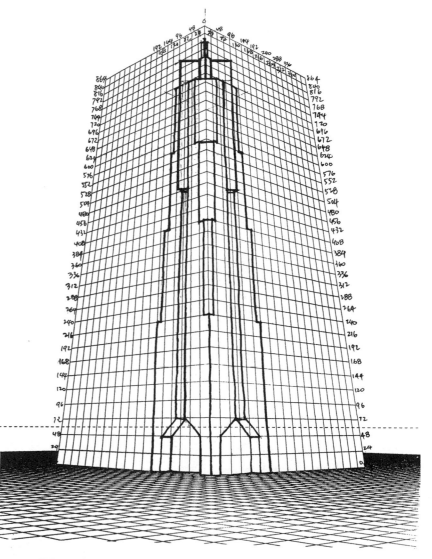

Figure 5-9

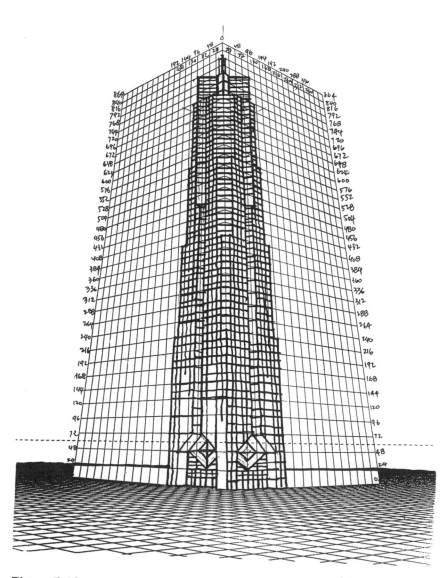

Figure 5-10

Figure 5-11

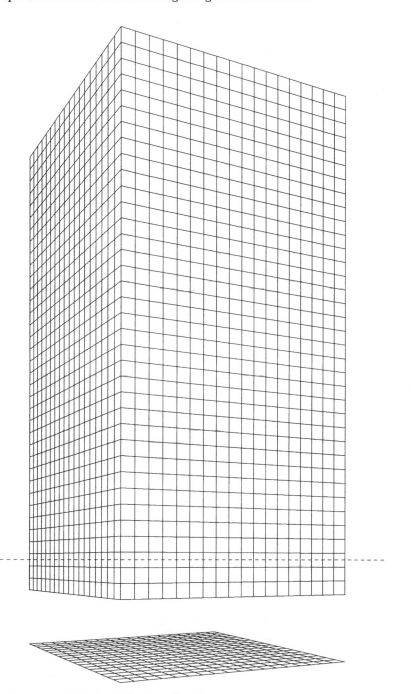

Exterior example 1, view 1, horizon line 5.

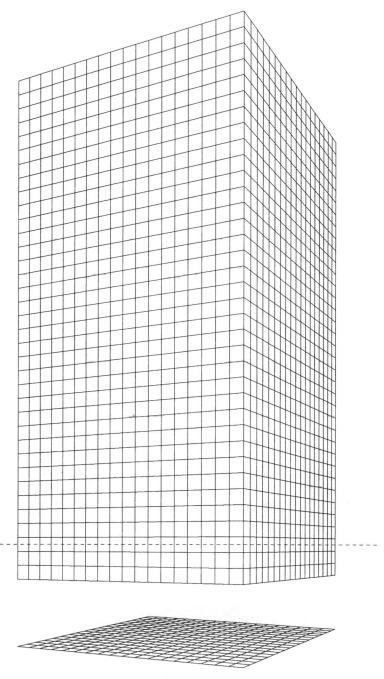

Exterior example 1, view 5, horizon line 5.

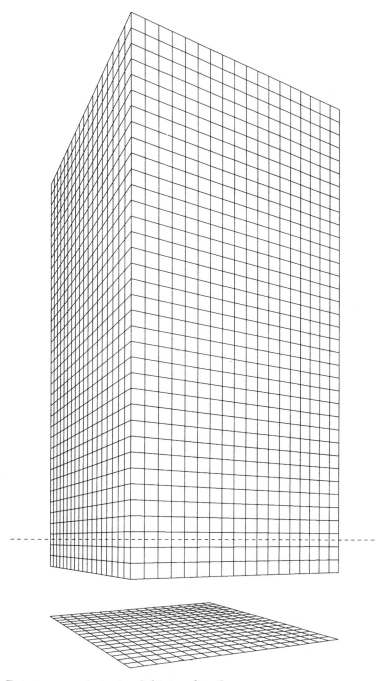

Exterior example 1, view 6, horizon line 5.

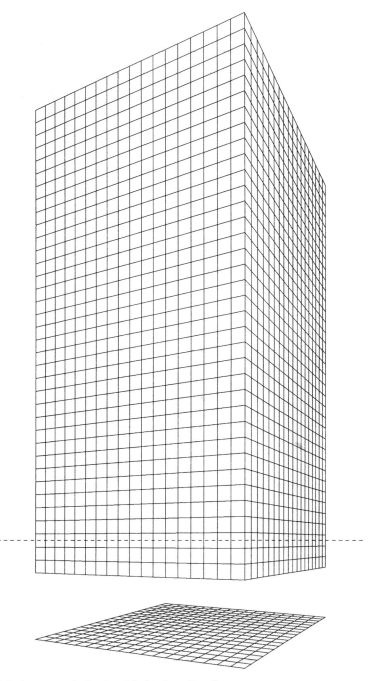

Exterior example 1, view 10, horizon line 5.

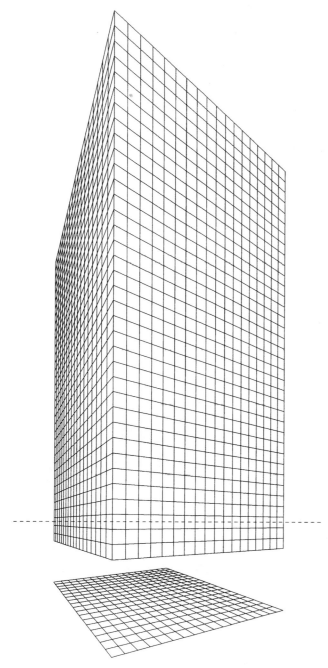

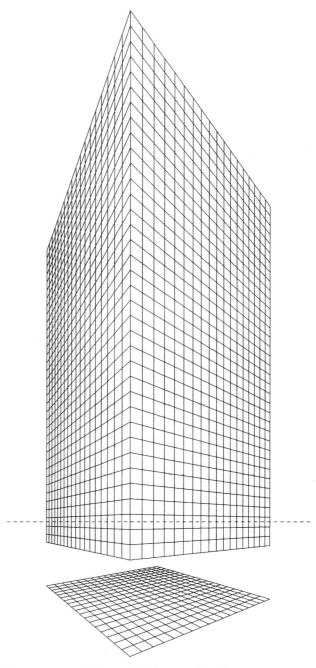

Exterior example 1, view 11, horizon line 5.

Exterior example 1, view 12, horizon line 5.

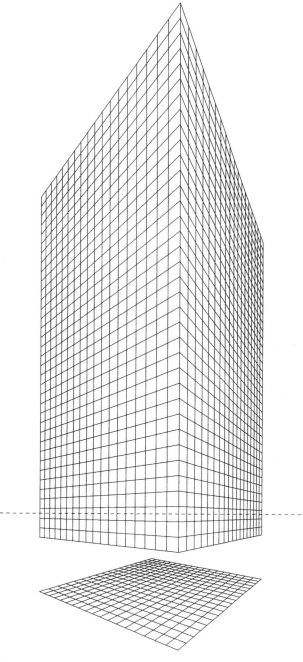

Exterior example 1, view 14, horizon line 5.

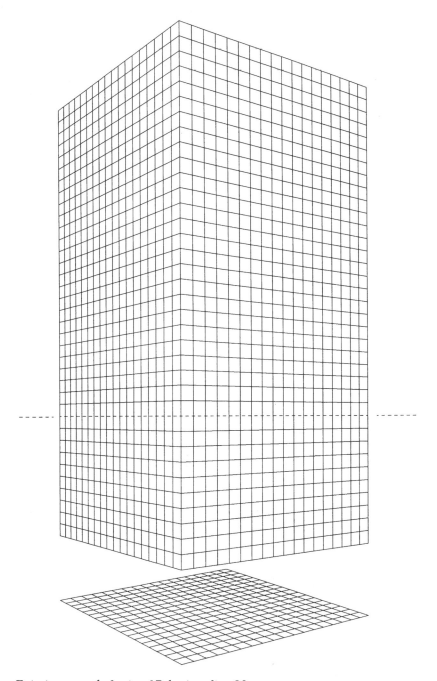

Exterior example 1, view 17, horizon line 20.

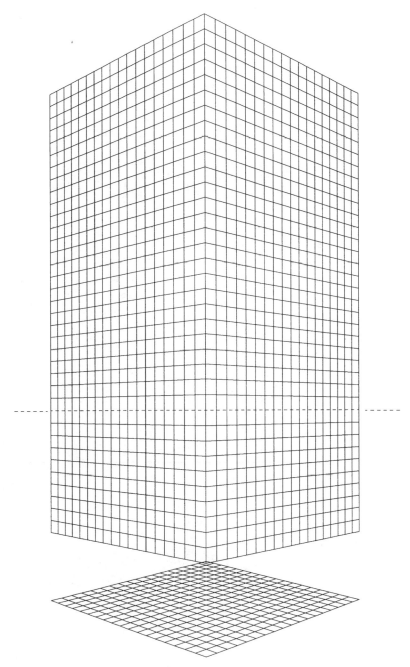

Exterior example 1, view 18, horizon line 20.

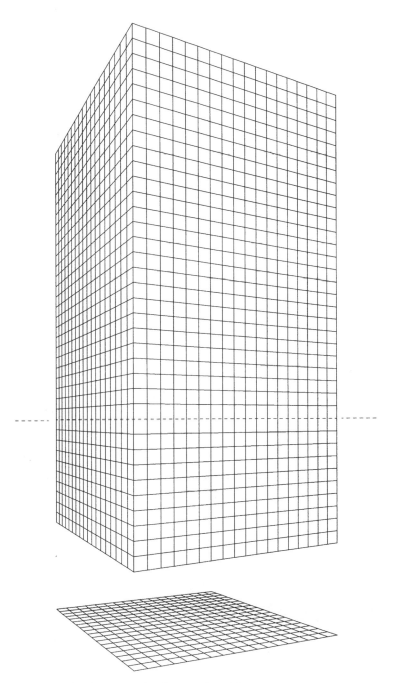

Exterior example 1, view 21, horizon line 20.

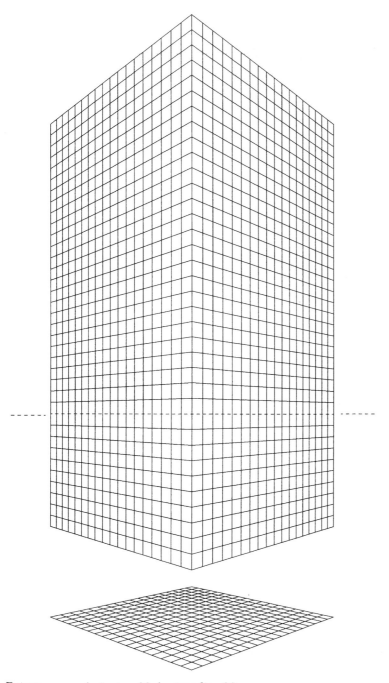

Exterior example 1, view 23, horizon line 20.

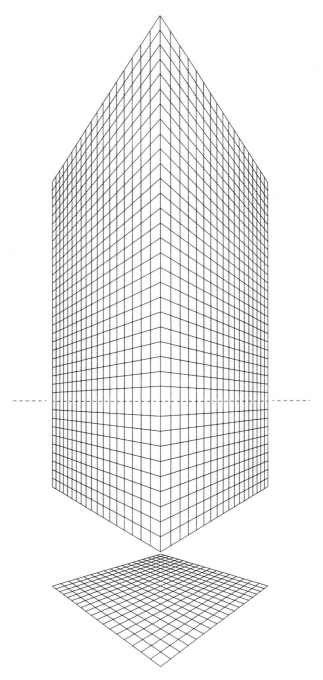

Exterior example 1, view 28, horizon line 20.

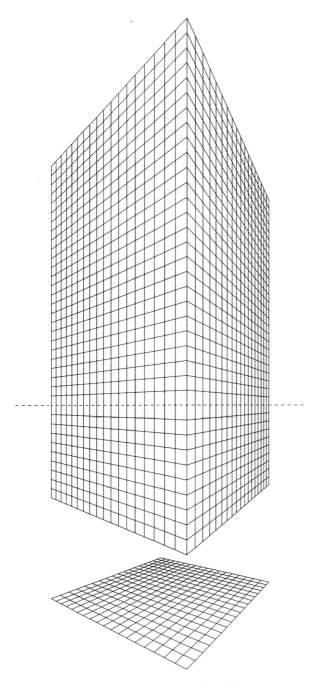

Exterior example 1, view 29, horizon line 20.

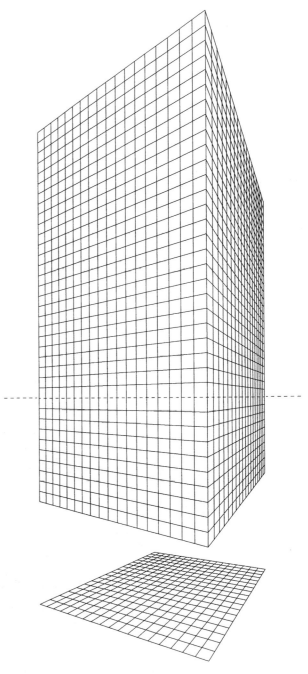

Exterior example 1, view 30, horizon line 20.

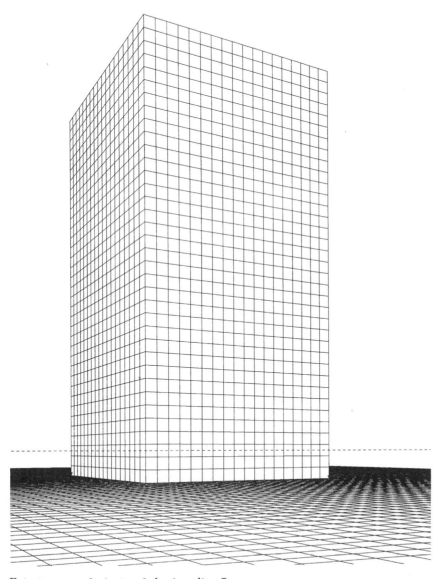

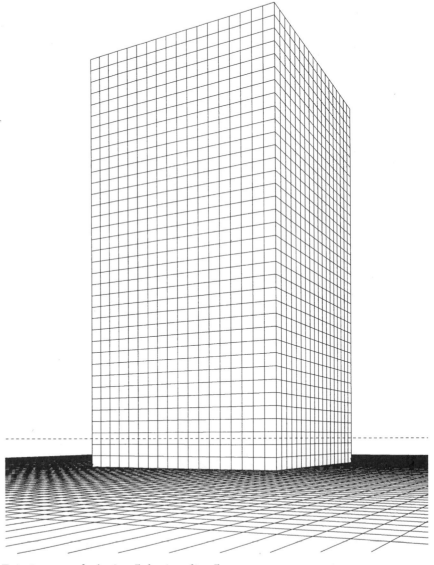

Exterior example 4, view 1, horizon line 5.

Exterior example 4, view 5, horizon line 5.

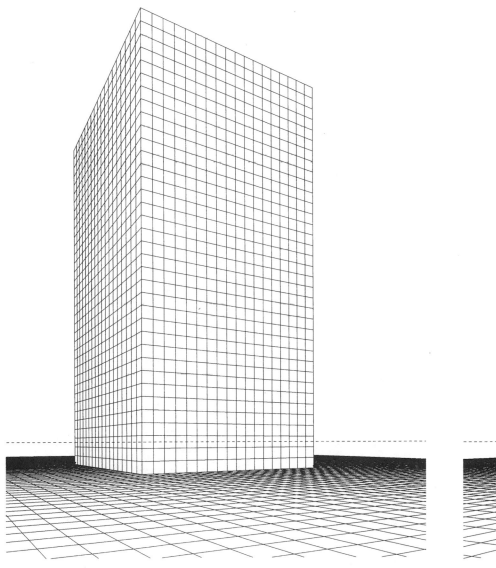

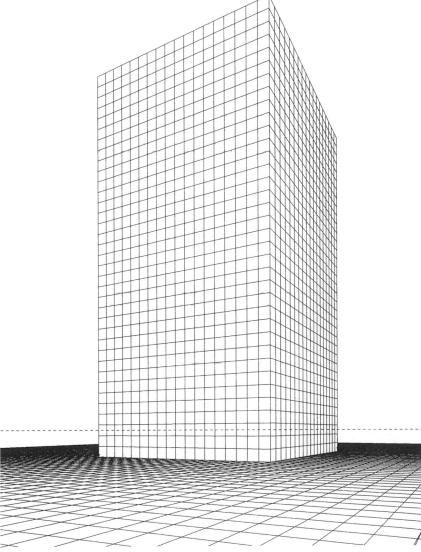

Exterior example 4, view 6, horizon line 5.

Exterior example 4, view 10, horizon line 5.

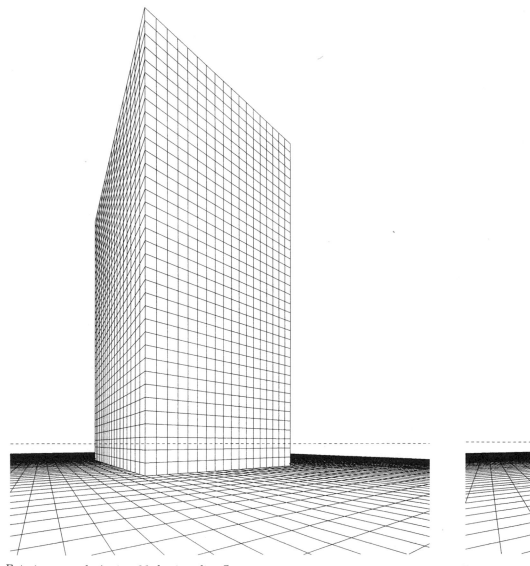

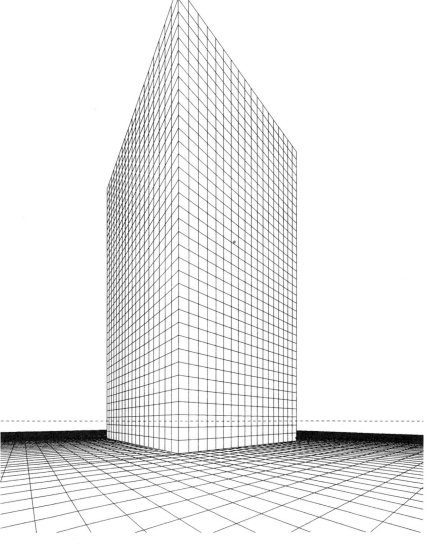

Exterior example 4, view 11, horizon line 5.

Exterior example 4, view 12, horizon line 5.

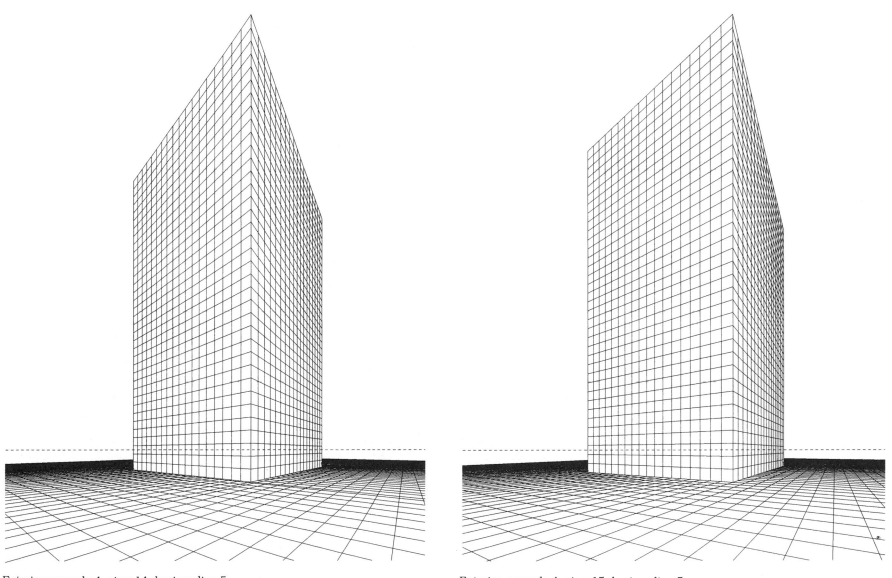

Exterior example 4, view 14, horizon line 5.

Exterior example 4, view 15, horizon line 5.

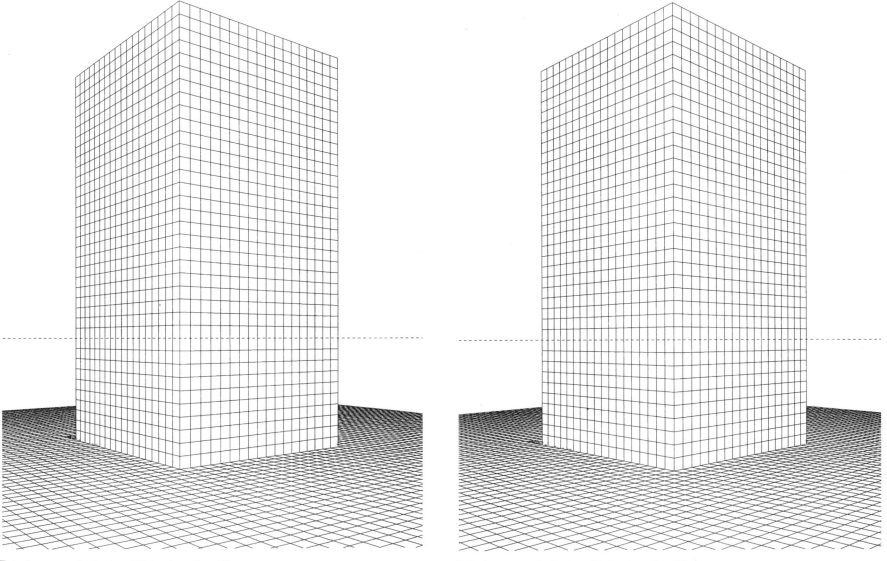

Exterior example 4, view 17, horizon line 20.   Exterior example 4, view 18, horizon line 20.

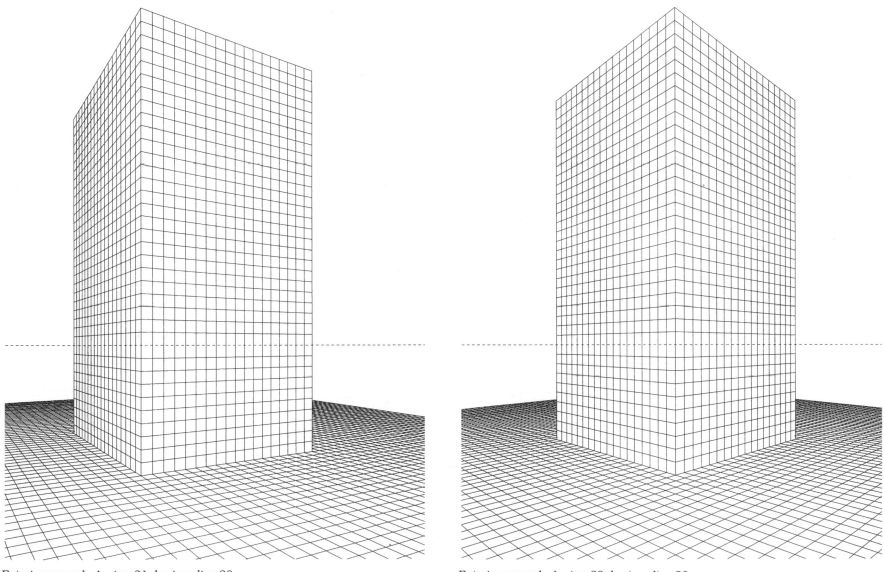

Exterior example 4, view 21, horizon line 20.

Exterior example 4, view 23, horizon line 20.

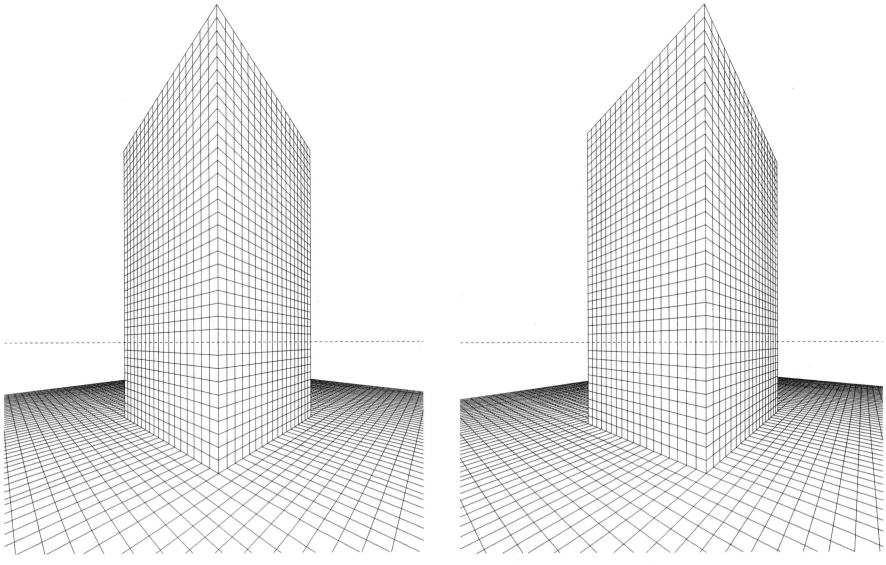

Exterior example 4, view 28, horizon line 20.

Exterior example 4, view 29, horizon line 20.

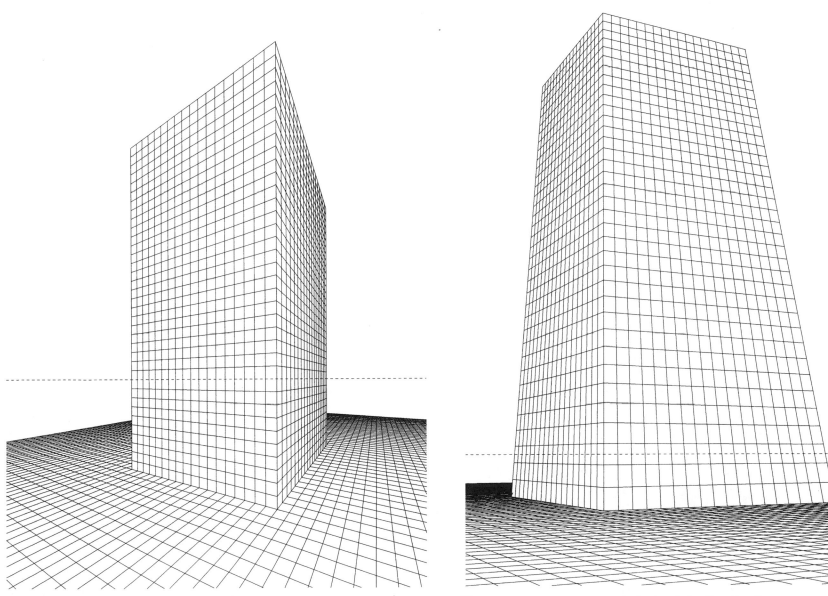

Exterior example 4, view 30, horizon line 20.

Three-point perspective example 1, view 1, horizon line 5.

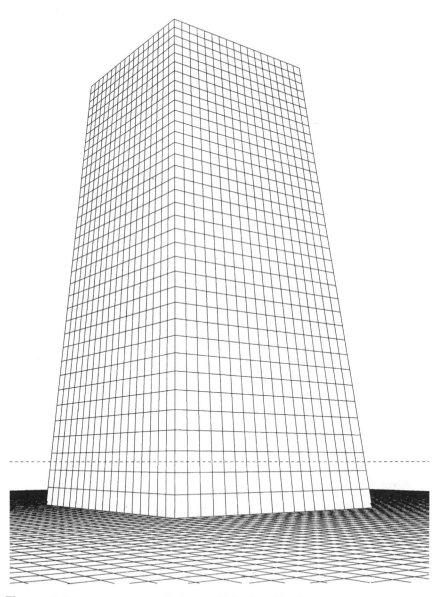

Three-point perspective example 1, view 2, horizon line 5.

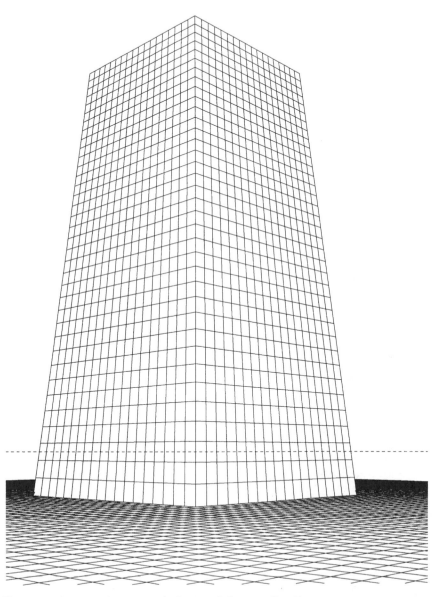

Three-point perspective example 1, view 3, horizon line 5.

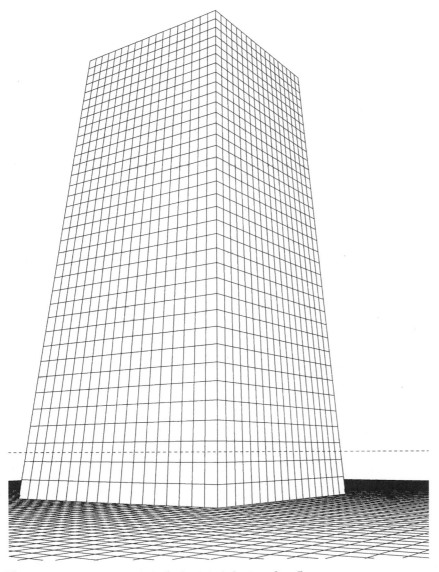

Three-point perspective example 1, view 4, horizon line 5.

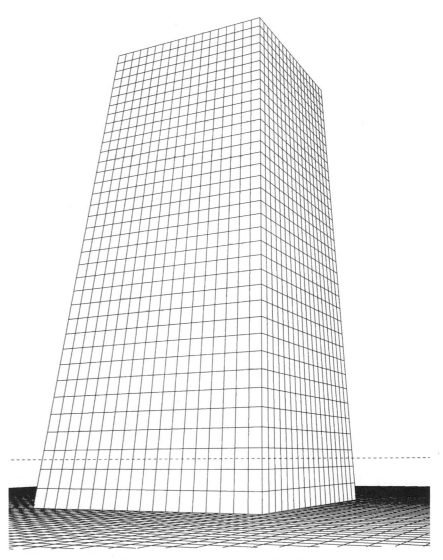

Three-point perspective example 1, view 5, horizon line 5.

Use of the Accompanying Diskette

The perspective grids in this book were created by using the modeling and rendering package of Sigma Design's ARRIS software. A three-dimensional cube with gridded surfaces was created, and a series of view angles (see Fig. 6-1) were established to allow for the creation of the individual grid views to be used in this book. The final perspective grids generated include the following:

Bird's-eye views. These grids represent a view of the gridded surfaces from above and are used most often for the development of site design perspectives.

Exterior views. These grids represent the views of the gridded surfaces on the exterior surfaces of the cube and are used mainly for development of exterior perspectives. Included among these grids are a range of building shapes from low-rise to mid-rise and high-rise. A set of grids using three-point perspective is also included for the taller buildings. Each final exterior grid comes in two formats—one with the floor plan grid for development of the building exterior and the other is a matching grid with the ground plane.

Interior views. These grids represent a series of views with 8-, 9-, 10-, and 12-unit interior heights. The use of these grids will enable the development of a wide range of interior perspectives.

Due to size limitations of the book, approximately 120 of the 300 grids have been printed in hard copy. All 300 grids have been included on the diskette. To archive the grids in a format that will allow them to be used on a number of computer-assisted design (CAD) systems, the grids have been translated to the DXF format. This will enable the reader to translate the grids to any CAD system that supports DXF.

The DXF files have been archived into a compressed file called GRIDS.EXE. This file is a self-exploding executable file which will expand to the following DXF files:

Bird's-eye (15 grids)

Bird's-eye-2 (15 grids)

Ext-1 (30 grids)

Ext-2 (30 grids)

Ext-3 (30 grids)

Ext-4 (30 grids)

Ext-5 (30 grids)

Ext-6 (30 grids)

3pt (10 grids)

Int-1 (18 grids)

Int-2 (18 grids)

Int-3 (18 grids)

Int-4 (18 grids)

To load the files onto your computer, insert the disk into the drive and copy the file GRIDS.EXE to your hard drive. Change the directory to the location where you copied this file on your hard drive and type in GRIDS.EXE and hit enter. The individual DXF files will then be created.

The process for translating the DXF files to drawing files compatible with your CAD software will require following the DXF-in instruction for your specific software. Each grid included in the above files is located on a separate layer of the drawing; for example, layer 1 in any of the drawings represents view 1, as indicated on the hard copy of the perspective grids. This system will enable the reader to locate and plot any grid at any size or rotation required. The grids are formatted to fit in an 8½ by 11 inch sheet size, as printed in this book, so an appropriate scale factor must be used to plot the grids at the size you require.

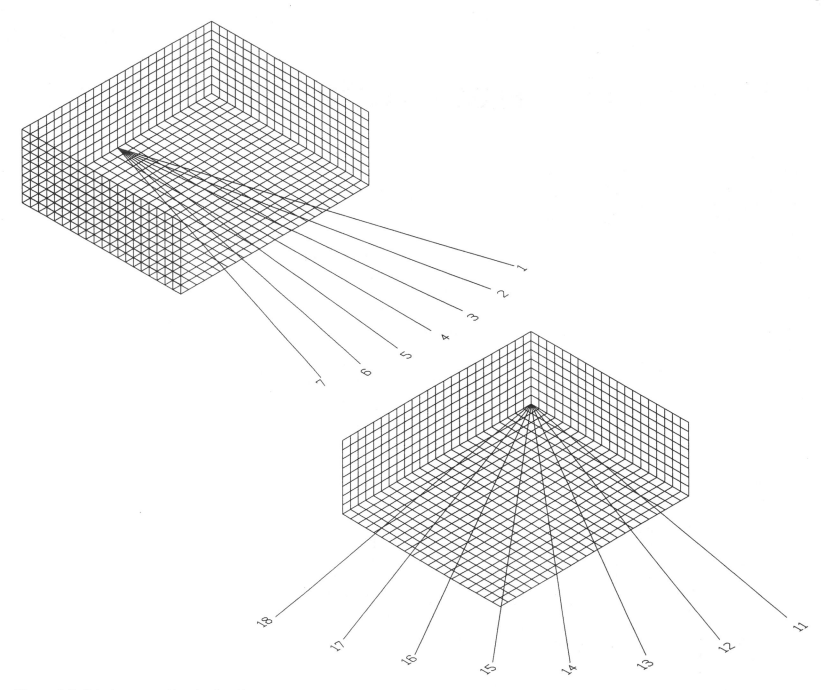

Figure 6-1. Interior perspective view locations.

ABOUT THE AUTHORS

JOHN CHEN, AIA, is a practicing architect and an associate professor in the School of Architecture and Planning at Howard University. He received a master of architecture degree from the University of California at Berkeley. In a professional career spanning more than 30 years, he has done many designs and presentations and has published more than 40 articles in the United States and abroad. He is the author of the book *Architecture in Pen and Ink*. He also trained students who have since won design communication awards.

WILLIAM T. COOPER, AIA, has been an architect practicing in the Baltimore-Washington area for the past 16 years. He received a bachelor of architecture degree from the University of Maryland at College Park. He has been actively involved with the use of CADD for the past 12 years and served as president and technical adviser of the National Capital ARRIS Users Group from 1990 to 1994. He is the founder of CADD Resources Management, a consulting firm which provides assistance in implementing technology for building design, development, construction, and facility management professionals.